Making Consultation Work:
the importance of process

Professor Phillip Beaumont
Professor Laurie Hunter

The Chartered Institute of Personnel and Development is the leading publisher of books and reports for personnel and training professionals, students, and all those concerned with the effective management of people at work.
For full details of all our titles, please contact the Publishing Department:

Tel.: 020 8612 6204
E-mail: publish@cipd.co.uk

The catalogue of all CIPD titles can be viewed on the CIPD website: www.cipd.co.uk/bookstore

For details of CIPD research projects:
www.cipd.co.uk/research

Making Consultation Work: the importance of process

P B Beaumont

L C Hunter

School of Business and Management, University of Glasgow

© Chartered Institute of Personnel and Development 2005

First published 2005

Cover design by Curve
Designed by Beacon GDT
Typeset by Paperweight
Printed in Great Britain by Short Run Press, Exeter

British Library Cataloguing in Publication Data:
A catalogue record for this book is available from the British Library

ISBN 1 84398 114 9

Chartered Institute of Personnel and Development
151 The Broadway, London SW19 1JQ

Tel.: 020 8612 6200
E-mail: www.cipd.co.uk

incorporated by Royal Charter: Registered charity no. 1079797.

Contents

Acknowledgements

Once again we would like to record our thanks to the managers, employees and union representatives who so generously gave of their time to provide the information reported here. A number of our practitioner colleagues, most notably Toni McAlindin and Sandra Stewart, helped provide us, in numerous conversations, with important insights and observations from the larger practitioner world. A number of our academic colleagues, namely Moira Fischbacher and Judy Pate, worked closely with us on one of the major cases reported here, for which we are most grateful.

Finally, a special word of thanks goes to Bob McKersie with whom we have had numerous pleasant and helpful conversations extending over many years. These have contributed enormously to our appreciation and understanding of the importance of the process of consultation.

Foreword

One of the biggest challenges employers face in informing and consulting with their employees in a meaningful manner is ensuring that the process of consultation is clearly understood across the organisation. This was one of the findings from the CIPD 2003 Research Report *Information and Consultation: from compliance to performance.* The report found that many organisations were unclear both about the meaning of consultation and what it really involves in practice.

As a result of the uncertainties among employers highlighted by this study the CIPD commissioned authors Professor Phil Beaumont and Professor Laurie Hunter to explore in more detail the issue of consultation and what it means in a business context.

This new Research Report for the CIPD is published as the Information and Consultation of Employees Regulations are about to come into force for organisations with 150 or more employees.

CIPD research shows that organisations that involve and engage their employees are likely to benefit through increased motivation and commitment. However, establishing meaningful arrangements for informing and consulting with employees is not easy to achieve. Consultation cannot be an empty process and must be underpinned by a genuine commitment from decision-makers to take account of employees' views before decisions that affect them are taken.

It is the quality of the process – the conversations that take place and the trust that is demonstrated – rather than the structure of the arrangements that will determine whether employees ultimately feel that their views have been heard.

It is essential that employers seeking to establish arrangements to inform and consult with their employees have a clear awareness of the issues that are key to effective consultation. Potential legal challenges to established information and consultation arrangements may well involve claims that the underlying process is not one of consultation.

Just as importantly, any anticipated organisational gains generated through effective information and consultation arrangements are only likely to occur if they are underpinned by an appropriate and relevant process of consultation.

The report is based on an analysis of a series of case studies involving employers, which have already established, or are attempting to establish, arrangements to inform and consult with their employees.

It demonstrates that there is a range of common key elements of consultation to address and these impact in different ways within different organisations. These components of consultation include whether unions are recognised, the business and economic position of the organisation and the nature of the employee relations climate. Tailoring, rather than the application of a single model or template, is essential.

Other key issues explored are the content of consultation, the timescales and history and the experience and expertise of the participants.

Beaumont and Hunter also emphasise that there is scope for considerable differences in interpretation within organisations over what consultation means. This can lead to differences in expectation between employer and employees over what the process can deliver.

The case studies cover a wide range of organisations, which are at different stages in the development of arrangements to inform and consult with employees. One of the key themes emerging from the case studies is the importance of having in place representatives who are able to exhibit the attitudes and behaviours of leaders rather than simply delegates, at least on certain occasions.

Another theme identified revolves around the issue of trust in the consultation process. Trust needs to exist:

- between constituents and their representatives,

- between the representatives directly engaged in the consultation process, and

- between the representatives and what is termed 'the larger organisational context'.

An organisation's employee relations history and the perceptions of employers and managers will also influence the consultation process. In addition, Beaumont and Hunter consider some of the specific challenges faced by larger organisations in developing trust in the consultation process.

The report identifies some common lessons learned from the case studies. These include the need for mutual agreement about what the process of consultation should involve. It also emphasises that meaningful consultation is an evolutionary process. Organisations must face up to challenges as they occur and learn from them in a positive manner to ensure that the process is strengthened rather than undermined over time.

The report delves beneath the surface of consultation and reveals that practitioners need to understand in some depth the particular issues that affect the process within their organisation if it is to add value to the business.

The CIPD's work on the links between people management and business performance highlights the critical importance of employee involvement and engagement through effective communication and consultation. There are no easy answers or quick fixes. It is not really about suggested models or structures, or really even about the 2005 legislation. The essence is in developing effective and trusted consultation processes tailored to suit the needs, goals and character of each organisation.

HR professionals have a vital role to play and a major opportunity to have an impact by helping to build and maintain effective consultation channels and processes. We hope examples and lessons learned in this report can help you to determine and deliver what is best for your organisation.

Ben Willmott
CIPD Adviser, Employee Relations

1 | Introduction

The initial research

In late 2003 the CIPD published our first stage research report which examined a number of 'early organisation moves' in relation to the introduction of the Information Disclosure and Consultation Regulations, the first implementation date being April 2005. Among the key findings of this report were the following:

◘ The presence (and often growth) of non-union employee numbers in many unionised organisations, where non-union employee representation arrangements had never existed, but where management now felt it was essential to provide for this.

◘ The need to align information disclosure and consultation arrangements with real decision-making structures in organisations, to close any gaps in this regard and to forge complementary linkages between multiple levels and mechanisms of consultation and information disclosure.

◘ The need to rethink decision-making timeframes, particularly when multiple layers or levels of management were involved, in an attempt to avoid, or at least minimise, the 'too early–too late' issues and problems raised by the introduction of new or reformed consultation and disclosure arrangements.

◘ The recognition that training for disclosure and consultation purposes is needed for management, as well as for employee representatives.

◘ The often uneasy relationship between negotiation and consultation which took a number of forms: the concern that the latter could become the former over time, or in a number of cases a real lack of understanding and appreciation of what the process of consultation involved in practice.

◘ Concern that unevenness throughout the organisation in various matters, such as unionisation levels, larger business strategy, technology, structures and culture, could pose a major difficulty for the development of a coherent and meaningful agenda for consultation and disclosure over time.

More generally, our overwhelming impression was that employers were concentrating on structural issues (eg numbers of representatives, constituencies of representatives) with much less attention being given to the all-important *process* of employee–management interaction, particularly centering around the far from clear-cut notion of 'consultation'. Accordingly, we urged organisations to:

◘ Recognise that consultation and information disclosure are very different processes.

◘ Take explicit account of the four 'pillars' of the notion of 'fair consultation':

  ◘ consult when proposals are still at a formative stage;

  ◘ ensure adequate information is provided as a basis on which to respond;

  ◘ provide adequate time in which to respond;

  ◘ ensure a 'conscientious consideration' of the response.

◘ Develop the accepted ground rules (and hence help align stakeholder expectations) of consultation via a prior process of 'consultation about consultation'.

'...there may be many organisations that will come late to reaching decisions on what steps they wish – or need – to take to comply with the legislation.'

Intervening developments

The draft regulations

In July 2003 the Government produced a Consultative Document on the Regulations, seeking responses to a number of outstanding issues, particularly:

1   the appropriate level of implementation (concerning undertakings, groups of undertakings, establishments),

2   the relationship of the new proposals to existing information and consultation requirements (eg collective redundancies), and

3   the relationship to collective agreements with trade unions.

An important outcome of this consultative exercise was recognition of the need for a clearer statement of Government intent in the form of a detailed set of guidance notes for practitioners, and a Draft version was issued by the DTI in July 2004. This effectively provides a near-final statement of the way the Regulations will be implemented, defining coverage, processes for setting up consultative arrangements, duty of cooperation, compliance and enforcement, and a number of other issues. For the purposes of this report, we adopt definitions and prescriptions as set out in the Draft. The existence of ACAS guidance on good practice for information and consultation is also important to note (go to www.acas.org.uk).

Our activities

In the interim between the completion of our first report and the commencement of research for the second stage, we were actively involved in speaking at a number of conferences, were involved in training sessions for management and employee representatives in a number of settings and provided advisory and facilitation contributions in several organisations. Some of the information and insights we gained from these activities are incorporated in later stages of this report, but more importantly they provided us with some guidance into what were emerging as important practical issues on which further research would be helpful.

In particular, we observed that a sizeable majority of practitioners were not proposing to try to put in place any new or revised arrangements prior to April 2005, on the grounds that they were waiting for more clarity in the final form of the Regulations and guidance notes, and that they were currently dealing with more pressing problems. A minority, however, had actively begun to develop new arrangements, which they saw as essential to meet particular needs in their own operational context, including the introduction of machinery or procedures that would improve their existing practice with respect to information provision and consultative practice. At the time of writing this report, we suspect that not too much has changed in this respect, which means that there may be many organisations that will come late to reaching decisions on what steps they wish – or need – to take to comply with the legislation.

This provides us with an ideal opportunity to provide, on the basis of our recent research, some practical guidance on a number of issues that seem to us to be critical to the operation of an effective information and consultation procedure. The approach we take differs from that set out in the Regulations and the associated guidance notes, which are essentially concerned with the legalistic issues and requirements, and relate much more to matters of setting up arrangements and structures than to matters of process. In that sense, the present report is complementary to the guidance notes and it is no part of our purpose to go over the ground covered by them.

The present study also differs significantly from our earlier report. We want particularly to concentrate on the process of consultation, reflecting our view that:

◘ the anticipated organisational gains from such arrangements are only likely to materialise if structures are underpinned by an appropriate and relevant process,

◘ any legal challenges to established arrangements may well involve claims that the underlying process is not one of consultation.

To develop this line of thinking, we established a set of explicit criteria for selecting cases for this study (drawing on some of our previous cases as well as adding new ones). It was important also for us to include not only cases where there was continuity from previous arrangements to new ones, but also cases where the issues of start-up from a zero base were being considered. The resultant case study information gave us considerable insight into two key questions:

◘ What were the parties seeking to achieve through the establishment or development of the consultation process?

◘ What seemed to be the driving or determining factors (or hindrances) in achieving the desired outcomes?

This approach provides the rationale for the way we present our findings here. Rather than provide simply a write-up of individual cases, we want to use the information obtained more purposefully, by using the case information to illustrate issues and themes arising under these two main headings.

In Chapter 2, we set out our approach to the research, which can also be regarded as a framework for analysis and decision-making. Chapter 3 explores the nature of the consultation process that the parties are seeking to establish, while Chapter 4 examines the factors influencing the motivation and ability to deliver the desired process. Chapter 5 selects a limited range of emerging issues requiring careful consideration by the parties, and Chapter 6 presents our summary and conclusions.

This report is likely to be of interest to anyone involved in improving consultation in the workplace. Wherever possible we use the experiences from the case studies to provide practical guidance on establishing and improving the actual processes of consultation and their outcome.

2 | Framework for research and decision-making

Introduction

In the academic and practitioner literature the 'process' aspects of employee consultation have been seriously underplayed in relation to the consideration of structural issues such as the composition and remit of consultative groups, the frequency of meetings, etc. This lack of attention to process would suggest that it is not important or that it is homogeneous. In our view, the converse is true: process is both critical to outcome and heterogeneous in character. By 'process' in this study we mean the series of steps leading to an outcome or decision, involving a social interaction between management and employees or their representatives with the aim of reaching or confirming a decision affecting the mutual interests of the parties.

This interaction will be subject to a wide range of influences, stemming in part from the structures and organisational arrangements in which consultation is embedded (and nothing we say should detract from the importance of sound structures and clarity of organisation), but also from the characteristics of the parties, the nature of the relationship between them, the sorts of issues they tackle in their agenda, and the values and expectations the parties bring to the consultative process. Further, the experience of being involved, directly or indirectly, in the process will create its own dynamic. In the process of information exchange and discussion to influence decisions, attitudes and perceptions will shift even in the course of a single meeting. In a recurrent consultative format, such as a works council, each individual consultative event (a meeting or communication between the parties) will have a future impact on attitudes and behaviour.

Components of process

To understand better how these various influences operate, we develop our analysis further, leading towards the development of our research tool, but also providing a basis for self-assessment by practitioners reviewing their consultative arrangements. We examine in turn:

- the environmental or structural conditions in which consultation is positioned,

- the nature of the substantive issues subject to consultation,

- the values and expectations brought by the parties to the consultation process,

- the stages of the consultative process.

Context: 'structural' conditions

These conditions can be divided into three groups: the parties, the structure and rules for consultation, and maturity and experience. The issues are posed as questions.

The parties

Does the organisation or undertaking have a union or unions recognised for collective bargaining purposes?

If there is no trade union present, there will be a need to agree a procedure for electing employee representatives[1], and once in place, the representatives may be both inexperienced in consultative skills and lacking in support and advice for their role. Where unions are already

> **'...if consultation is seen as a weak option or a management device to weaken negotiation, the contribution from consultation may be small and short-lived.'**

present, the support and advice of full-time union officers and the training resources available to the union are likely to produce greater 'know-how' and confidence on the part of the representatives. The existence of collective bargaining may also provide confidence (for both parties) in that there is an alternative channel of 'voice' that may be brought into play, or to which disputed issues may be referred at an appropriate stage. On the downside, if consultation is seen as a weak option or a management device to weaken negotiation, the contribution from consultation may be small and short-lived. The presence of more than one union, and particularly the existence of separate bargaining tables for different employee groups, will tend to add to the problems of achieving effective consultation.

What is the density of union membership and how evenly is it spread through the organisation?

Higher levels of union membership are likely to create greater union solidarity and support for the process, but this may be weakened if (as is common) the membership is unevenly spread through the organisation. This may make it more difficult to obtain a broadly proportional distribution of representatives from different parts of the organisation.

What is the business and economic position of the organisation?

A secure and stable business organisation is likely to be associated with more confident managers and greater clarity of company policies. Conversely, where the business context is fragile or volatile (eg reflecting technological or market changes), the tensions within the process are likely to be higher, more uncertainty will be apparent, and the consultation process may be more inhibited and limited.

Structures

What is the structure of the consultative mechanism?

In structural terms, it is likely to matter whether there is a single or dual channel for employee representation. In unionised establishments there may be separate bargaining units for different employee groups, and just as unions sometimes find it difficult to sit at a single bargaining table with other unions, so there may be reluctance to participate in a single consultative committee. But there is also the consideration (specifically required under the I & C legislation) that non-union employees should have equivalent access to information and to consultative mechanisms; and some unions have shown reluctance to participate in a single integrated consultation group. Where more than one consultative mechanism exists, there is greater likelihood of variations in the agenda and its handling, more demands on management time and greater complexity in maintaining harmony and equality of treatment between the channels.

A further aspect of structure may arise in multi-site organisations, where there may be provision for both site-level and higher level consultation committees. This may lead to the need to define clearly what can be discussed at each level, and how articulation between the levels is to be managed. While this tiered arrangement is no doubt necessary (especially if consultation is to be carried out at 'appropriate' levels in the organisation[2]), it undoubtedly adds a further layer of complexity to the process and requires careful management by both parties.

Relationships, maturity and trust

The issues raised here, though quite different in character from the above, are nevertheless an

> '**...where the norm is one of trust and cooperation, there is greater scope for an integrative, problem-solving approach.**'

essential part of the operating context. They introduce the issue of trust, which will play a large part in our subsequent cases and discussion.

Is the underlying relationship between the parties conflictual or consensual?

In consultation, as in bargaining, specific issues can throw up unexpected results. Occasionally, parties accustomed to mistrust and aggressive attitudes can find themselves united; and conversely, a well-established trust relationship can threaten to run off the rails. However, the parties will enter any specific consultative event or cycle with an expectation as to the degree of harmony or conflict likely to be displayed. It is almost inevitable that where conflictual relations are the norm and mistrust is entrenched, the consultative process will either be trivialised (because the parties recognise the real outcome will be determined elsewhere) or prove difficult to lead into areas where mutual accommodation can be reached. Conversely, where the norm is one of trust and cooperation, there is greater scope for an integrative, problem-solving approach.

Our later discussion will take this issue much further, but in the meantime it is important to note that there is much more at stake than simply the relationship between the management and employee representatives in a consultative forum. We take the view that too little attention has been given to:

◘ The different dimensions of the trust relationship (not only management – employee representatives, but also management – employees, and employees – representatives): trust and good working relations at representative level may not be mirrored in the attitudes of constituents.

◘ What are the key determinants of trust, and to what extent are they under the control of the representatives directly involved in the consultation process? The nexus of trust relationships at any time will almost inevitably reflect the historical baggage attaching to the relationship, as well as the current status and activity.

Since there are very strong grounds for believing that the degree of trust among the parties is critical to the conduct and outcome of consultation, this has to be an important point of focus in our subsequent analysis.

How mature is the consultation procedure, and how experienced are the participants in the process?

A long-established procedure will tend to have generated mutual understandings and ways of handling business, which will ease the processing of the agenda, in contrast to newly established mechanisms that are likely to experience teething problems. This need not affect the quality of the 'output', however. Old procedures may have allowed the process to get into a rut, while new procedures may generate enthusiasm and high commitment to the activity. Similar issues arise with respect to the participants. Those who are old hands in the process will be more able to read the signals in exchanges between the parties: new participants will have to learn how to read what is happening. Both new and old may produce positive or negative outcomes.

What training in consultative (and bargaining) roles has been provided to management and employee representatives?

The skills required in consultation are often taken for granted, especially where representatives

> '...the skill of effective consultation is subtly different from that of negotiation and increasingly companies are providing training in the consultative role for their employees...'

already have experience of bargaining. However, the skill of effective consultation is subtly different from that of negotiation and increasingly companies are providing training in the consultative role for their employees; where unions are present they too are able to provide training for members. There is increasing attention also to training management to handle consultative and information communication roles, though this is far from universal. Two criteria would seem to be important here in relation to the performance of the process. First, how far is the training provided aligned to the specific context of the organisation? And second, to what extent is *joint* training undertaken (involving management and employee representatives working together), rather than separation of training channels? The more aligned the training to company circumstances, and the more that joint training is undertaken, the greater would seem to be the chances of effective interaction and communication.[3]

The content of consultation

Our second main proposition is that the content of consultation – the scope and significance of the issues under discussion – will have considerable bearing on the effectiveness of the process.

The obvious polarisation is between issues that are 'routine' and those that can be described as in some way extraordinary – which would include 'crisis' events such as a threatened site closure or major change in technology or working practices. By routine items, we mean consultation such as will take place in scheduled meetings of JCCs established as an ongoing vehicle for employee voice in an organisation. These meetings are recurrent events in the annual cycle of organisational activities, providing an agreed, constitutionally based opportunity for the

exchange of information and opinion within the management–employee relationship. There are likely to be some regular agenda items: the 1998 WER Survey identified the most common issues as working practices (88 per cent of establishments) health and safety (86 per cent), welfare services and facilities (83 per cent) and future workplace plans (also 83 per cent). (Cully, *et al*, 1999, p 101.) But other issues such as pay matters, training and production and quality performance may well be regular items. The main point is that these would be items that both parties could anticipate as recurrent agenda items in a continuing dialogue.

This contrasts with the other extreme when some critical event arrives, such as management giving notice about a site closure or a major reorganisation. Such an issue is likely to arrive without much warning and may loom as a 'crisis' for management and employees. The *process* of consultation in these extreme positions is likely to be different from the routine, to be much more tense and emotive, more demanding in terms of time pressures and subject to a more intense focus.

Perhaps, though, it would be wrong to see the reality through this polarised perspective. In practice, any agenda is likely to contain items of different immediacy and criticality, and so may generate different approaches to the handling of the business. Furthermore, it is not necessarily the case that either party would *want* to work regularly in either the routine or the crisis mode. From the point of view of constructive consultation, it may be much preferable to give an *in-depth focus* to key issues before they develop into difficulties or to problems that could be tackled cooperatively. In other words, rather than letting the agenda choose itself, either as routine or emergency, the skilful (joint) management of the agenda may be a preferable approach.

Values and expectations

Few would disagree with the proposition that the parties committing themselves to a consultative process should do so with a full and equal understanding of the purpose. Without that, there is a high risk that the parties will enter into consultation (and information provision more generally) with different expectations, and if that occurs, the stage is set for disappointment and disillusion. A fundamental aspect of this is how the parties interpret consultation.

A not uncommon scenario is that employees expect that consultation will provide them with an opportunity to change management's mind. More than this, they may expect that management *will* change its mind or at least make some concessions. But management, in engaging in consultation, may simply believe that it is desirable that employees should have a chance to express their views, without any commitment to changing the decision. So long as consultation is dealing with minor issues, this difference may not matter, but when a major issue arises and management will not change its intentions in the face of resistance and counter-argument from the employee representatives, the scene is set for a sense of let-down, even a sense of betrayal. This in turn will impact on the trust relationship between the parties, and hence on future relationships, and rebuilding trust may be a long term process.

If we accept that full and equal understanding of purpose is necessary for a sound approach to consultation, it is important to recognise the various shades of meaning that can be attached to it. Some initial guidance is given in the DTI consultative paper (2003) as shown below.

The management must consult the I & C Committee on the matters in paragraph (iii) (b) and (c) above [*referring to different types of issue*]

- while ensuring that the timing, method and content of the consultation are appropriate;

- on the basis of the information supplied by the management and of the opinion which the committee is entitled to formulate, and

- in such a way as to enable the committee to meet with the relevant level of management and obtain a reasoned response to any such opinion.

In relation to decisions under (iii) (c) above, consultation must take place with a view to reaching agreement on decision-taking within the scope of management's powers'. (DTI 2003, p10).

The clear intention is that legislation will set different requirements for consultation according to the substantive issue in question. In the 'normal' case, consultation will allow for reasoned response only. This seems to treat consultation as an end in itself – there should be employee voice and there should be a reasoned response from the employer. But when it comes to matters under (iii) (c), (ie decisions likely to lead to substantial changes in work organisation or in contractual relations), the end becomes the more exacting one of aiming to reach agreement on decision-taking within the scope of management at the appropriate level[4]. However, the 2004 Draft Guidance Notes from the DTI observe that

this does not mean that the employer is obliged to follow the I & C representatives' opinion or to reach agreement with them. Consultation is not negotiation, bargaining or co-decision-making.
(DTI 2004, p74)

To provide some clarity on this, we have defined a spectrum of alternative avenues for employee voice which incorporate some options for consultation (see Table 1).

Taking information provision as the base, we proceed through the two forms of consultation envisaged in the DTI paper, and on to negotiation and co-determination, from which consultation is conceptually separate. For the purposes of our research, we also included two variants on the consultative process:

◘ problem-solving consultation, in which the parties meet to exchange views on current or imminent problems affecting the employment

Table 1 | Spectrum of management–employee interaction[5]

Information provision	Consultation – exchange of views (reciprocal)	Consultation – with view to reaching agreement	Negotiation	Co-determination
The main purpose is to allow one party to convey information to the other, to keep the other party informed about matters of current interest and to have a shared knowledge base as a reference point, eg in a meeting of management and employees (or representatives), management shares proposals with employees, but does not expect that employees will exercise 'voice'. Such information can also be provided through print documents, intranet communications, etc.	Before decision is finalised, proposals are discussed with the other party, providing opportunity for the partner's views and concerns to be represented and seriously considered on a mutual basis. There is explicit opportunity for 'voice' and an opportunity for mutual participation in the decision process.	The parties proceed as for reciprocal consultation, but the explicit purpose is to reach an agreed decision.	The purpose is to reach an outcome acceptable to both parties by satisfying their minimum requirements through a process of bargaining.	Decision-taking is not the prerogative of management but subject to joint agreement by management and employee representatives.

relationship. Here the intention is to develop a mutual understanding of the issues and if possible to agree a path or consensus approach to resolving them

◘ quasi-bargaining, in which the parties in a consultative context engage in preliminary stages of bargaining, such as clarification of positions, signalling likely reaction to hypothetical proposals or counter-proposals, and generally clearing the ground for a formal negotiation to pick up and take forward. (This may occur because formal constitutional arrangements or agreements preclude bargaining except in a recognised bargaining forum).

With at least four different types of consultation between the straightforward provision of information and the standard bargaining process, there is considerable scope for misunderstanding between (and within) the parties of what consultation is to mean in the specific context. Our earlier work (Beaumont and Hunter, 2003) suggests that parties do have different expectations when they enter into consultative arrangements (conflicting purpose or beliefs) and that those who are consulted are frequently at a loss to know what is involved and where the boundaries are to be drawn. For example, many employees are unclear why they are consulted on some issues but not on others, revealing a lack of clarity of purpose.

We can conclude, then, that there is considerable scope for misunderstanding of what consultation may involve, and there is a real need to ensure that the parties fully understand the scope and limitations of the form of consultation into which they are entering. Without that, the opportunity for confusion and loss of trust in the process is considerable.

Stages of consultation

Finally, we come to the dimension of process that provides insight into the steps that may be involved in the conduct of consultation. There is no blueprint, and depending on the issue, the context and indeed the whole set of influences discussed above, the number of stages and their composition may vary considerably. However, some hypothetical development of stages in a normal case can be suggested on the basis of observation and case studies. We assume a scenario in which a routine quarterly meeting of a well established JCC or Works council is imminent, and there are no expectations of any 'surprises'.

a. The parties would presumably engage in some form of preparatory activity, either by suggesting items for the agenda or agreeing an agenda circulated for comment. Depending on local practice, both management and employee representatives may arrange to have some preliminary *intra-party* discussion of the items identified to determine their respective positions, particularly where at least one item is possibly contentious. This preparation will be coloured by their appreciation of the prevailing state conditions, their expectation of the positioning and approach of the other party, and the normal purpose of consultation according to existing local practice. Just as in the approach to a negotiation, the intra-party discussion will allow individuals to have their say, enabling the leading spokesperson to develop a sense of the emerging reference and priorities of the group members, and if necessary to have some sense of an appropriate tactical positioning and response.

b. The meeting itself will open up an inter-party dialogue, with much depending again on the local culture (eg the degree of formality,

'Ultimately much depends on the importance attached to the issue by the parties, and on their motivation to have a real influence on what is to be done.'

whether open discussion or channelled through principal speakers, etc). Genuinely routine items may lead only to a few informational exchanges and clarifications, which may result in the item continuing on the agenda or some agreement on next steps being agreed. More contentious or non-trivial items with non-obvious solutions are likely to lead to a more intensive process of information exchange, which will seek to develop a fuller understanding of the position of both sides and an appreciation of where differences arise between them.

c. With such contentious issues, or issues that motivate the parties to seek a cooperative solution, the next stage will be a more systematic assembly of the information, testing for understanding and enabling doubts and reservations to be expressed. In effect, both sides will use this as a means of conveying a picture of their own preferences on the issues (whether that is a true reflection or a tactical presentation will be open to interpretation) and starting to identify really significant differences between the two positions. Both sides may probe to determine true resistance points and try to detect areas where some concession is possible.

d. These gaps between the sides will presumably have to be closed through discussion and concession if the issue is to be resolved. Much will now depend on the underlying relationship between the parties. In a conflictual context, the process of working towards an agreed solution may be difficult and protracted and indeed may lead to no real changes in position, simply a confirmation that an agreed solution is not going to be reached. Alternatively, in a more cooperative, problem-solving format, the stage may be set for a possibly longer-term

process of working together to find a solution. Where training has been provided on joint problem-solving or win–win bargaining techniques, there will be a common understanding of the stages that follow, and the item may thus be agreed as one that will continue on the agenda for some time, with further information and research being conducted out of committee. Problem-solving approaches without training will inevitably be more messy and confused, but may still lead to progress, if not final agreement.

e. The outcomes will range from no change in management's position, through minor changes in detail or more significant shifts of position, to a more thorough-going joint analysis over a period that leads either to a cooperative solution or to a stage at which bargaining over distributional issues can be determined. In multi-tier consultative arrangements, the issue may be passed to a higher level for further consideration.

This is, of course, an idealised picture of events and the actual process may appear much less ordered and more confused at any stage. Nor should one discount the effect of 'off-committee' manoeuvrings, such as the issuing by management of letters to individual employees (direct communication), staff briefings from management, or press releases; while on the staff side, union officers or representatives at other company sites may be consulted. Ultimately much depends on the importance attached to the issue by the parties, and on their motivation to have a real influence on what is to be done. In emergency situations, of course, the pressures will be much more immediate and urgent, representatives will be subject to questioning and advice from fellow employees or managerial colleagues and outcomes may be traumatic for one or both parties.

Our research on process

Using this analysis, we developed a checklist (see page 15) that would allow us to capture systematically the main characteristics of each of our case study organisations. There was no attempt to use this as a survey instrument. Rather it was used during interviews to cover a common range of issues. Many of the points generated considerable discussion, reflected in our later case material. Not all the points were relevant in each case: eg, where no consultative mechanism was yet in place, there was no case experience to be reported. But in the start-up cases, this approach served as a useful guide to considering the sorts of issues that would need to be taken into account in the formulation of a new consultative mechanism and you may find it a useful tool to help you review your own consultative arrangements.

We developed case information for 14 companies, chosen after contact with a wider range of companies about which we had information on how they had progressed in creating or adapting their approach to consultation. Wherever possible, we chose organisations that promised to offer an insight into different aspects of the consultation experience. Some of these were cases we had visited in the first stage of our research, others were new cases added because we felt they could illustrate some interesting angle on process. Table 2 on page 14 provides an overview summary of the case study organisations in the report and some of the key themes.

Although most of our cases focused on organisations that already had a form of consultation in operation, we also chose to include some that were in the very early stages of preparation, since we believed that their thinking would be useful in providing pointers to the many other companies that have yet to face up to the challenge of developing consultative mechanisms. The criteria used in choosing to continue existing cases and for adding new cases are listed below. The variety in terms of type and size of organisation, sector and situation should hopefully give you plenty of ideas to apply to your own situation.

Criteria for continuing cases and adding new cases

1   There had to have been some *tangible* progress or developments on the subject area since we had finished the first stage of the research, or were apparent in the new cases.

2   These tangible developments had to have involved, at least to some extent, the sort of process-related issues which we were particularly interested in, and which we have outlined in this chapter*.

3   Each case should have a clear, central theme, with ideally not too much duplication of these themes.

4   We sought examples (as far as possible) from all four of our original case study categories: in relation to EWCs; building on existing arrangements; partnership; no prior history or experience of direct and/or representative arrangements.

*   This was our *ideal* list of criteria. In practice, the major practical difficulty we experienced was obtaining cases where sufficient meetings had taken place to obtain information on the 'process in action'. (As indicated in Chapter 6 this is a priority for future research.)

Table 2 | Summary of case characteristics

COMPANY	NEW CASE	UNION RECOGNITION	SIZE	NO. OF RESPONDENTS	EMPLOYEE RELATIONSHIP	THEME(S)
CHILDCARE TRUST		No	Medium	Multiple	Consensual	Start-up: finding reps
COMMUNICATIONS		Yes	Large	Multiple	Conflictual	Complex consultation
DRINKS CO		Yes	Large	Multiple	Mixed	Training for reps
ELECTRONICS		No	Medium	Multiple	Consensual	More proactive reps
ENGINEERING		Yes	Large	Multiple	Mixed	Strategic shock
IT SERVICES		Yes	Large	Single	Variable	Business alignment
POWERCO		Yes	Large	Single	Moving toward consensual	Complex consultation
PROFESSIONAL	New	No	Medium	Multiple	Consensual	Zero base start-up
PUBLIC SECTOR (NO 2)	New	Yes	Large	Multiple	Mixed	Passive resistance
SOFT DRINKS	New	Yes	Large	Multiple	Positive, unfulfilled	Alignment
SOFTWARE	New	No	Medium	Single	Neutral	Zero base start-up
TELECOM	New	Yes	Large	Multiple	Robust and constructive	Complex consultation
TVCO	New	Yes (part)	Large	Single	Variable	Alignment: mgt. learning about consultation
PUBLIC SECTOR (NO 1)	New	Yes	Large	Multiple	Variable	Establishing ground rules

Finally in concluding this chapter, and before we turn to our case study material, we want to briefly highlight two research studies which have separately emphasised the importance of focusing on the nature of the consultation process. The first of these studies is the second stage of the CIPD-funded research project on organisational restructuring (Mayer, Smith and Whittington, 2004). For our purposes, their most salient findings were that:

◘ While employees were typically kept informed about the objectives and progress of re-organisation, very few organisations allowed employees significant influence on the process.

◘ However, it was only by combining feedback and questions with real involvement that positive employee-related performance outcomes were achieved.

The second study was a case study review of current practice on information disclosure and consultation in Ireland. This study by the National centre for Partnership and Performance (2004) variously concluded that:

◘ management were more at ease with informing than consulting,

◘ consultation was less prevalent in the early planning stages of organisational decision-making compared to the mid-planning and implementation phases, and

◘ *...the key to more effective informing and consulting lies not so much in the institutional arrangements that are adopted* per se *as in the context, manner and spirit in which they are introduced and progressed.*

(2004, p8)

Checklist: Key factors affecting the process of consultation

1   'State' conditions

◘ union(s) recognised (or otherwise present)

◘ union density and evenness of spread

◘ summary position of business (stability *vs* change)

◘ any significant changes in last year? – consultation structure:

  – single or dual channel (union and non-union separated?)
  – single or multiple tiers
  – degree of formality of proceedings,
  – communications patterns in committee
    (eg mainly through spokespersons or all participating in discussion?)

◘ perception of relations – conflictual or consensual

◘ high/low/ or medium level of mutual trust

  – between employee reps and management
  – between employees and management

◘ age of consultative arrangement

◘ consultative experience of key participants (recent or well-experienced?)

◘ nature and extent of consultation training, especially whether:

– joint training for management and employees
– training for employees only
– training in problem-solving or win–win bargaining techniques

2   Substantive issues

◘ is recent experience of consultation largely routine?

◘ any recent experience of non-routine or emergency events? eg redundancy, closure

◘ any experience of in-depth issues being tackled or use of problem-solving approach?

3   Purposes

◘ Is consultation seen as means or end?

◘ How far do parties share this understanding?

◘ Has it been explicitly addressed/reviewed?

◘ Perception of purpose: **(see Table 3 opposite)** – which best fits your situation?

4   Stages

◘ How is *routine* business handled in committee? (stages): perceptions of how each party prepares for and behaves in consultation.

◘ If experience of *non-routine* or problem-solving cooperative approaches to issues, provide account of process/stages.

◘ Perceptions of outcomes: expected extent of movement in positions, concessions – eg very flexible/fairly resistant/rigid.

◘ Perception of feedback effects on future process.

Table 3 | The purposes of consultation

Normal type of consultation	Definition	Comments
Reciprocal	Before decisions are finalised, the proposals are discussed with the other party, providing opportunity for the partner's views and concerns to be represented and seriously considered on a mutual basis.	
'Directed'	The parties proceed as for reciprocal consultation, but where the explicit or required purpose is to reach agreement on decision-taking.	
Problem-solving (win–win)	The parties meet to exchange views on current or imminent problems affecting the employment relationship. Here the intention is to develop a mutual understanding of the issues and, if possible, to agree a path or consensus approach to resolving them.	
'Near-bargaining'	The parties engage in preliminary stages of bargaining (eg because formal constitutional arrangements or agreements preclude bargaining except in a recognised bargaining forum), such as clarification of positions, signalling likely reaction to hypothetical proposals or counter-proposals, and generally clearing the ground for a formal negotiation to pick up and take forward.	

Endnotes

1   See Draft Guidance on the Information and Consultation Regulations, paras 30-31, 39

2   See Draft Guidance on the Information and Consultation Regulations, para 32

3   One possible caveat to attach here is that an organisation may want to carefully consider whether they should begin with joint training, as opposed to move to joint training over time.

4   It is worth noting that 'aiming to reach agreement' appears in the collective redundancies regulations and thus pre-dates these regulations.

5   We are grateful to Diane Sinclair for suggesting this approach.

3 | The nature of the consultative process in practice

Introduction

This chapter draws on our case materials to illustrate how organisations are tackling aspects of the consultation process. There are two broad categories. First, there are organisations starting from a zero base, with little or no experience of consultation other than *ad hoc* events. Second, there are organisations that have already established procedures but, for a wide range of reasons, wish to modify or develop their current approach.

In either case, the decision to 'do something' about consultation leads on to four further steps:

◘ arranging for representatives to be elected,

◘ defining and agreeing the purposes of consultation,

◘ determining the sort of agenda items to be dealt with in consultation and agreeing aspirations,

◘ deciding how outcomes of the process are to be disseminated and what actions are needed.

Starting from a zero base

Three cases serve to illustrate the start-up problem: a private sector software design and engineering company (Software), a professional firm (Professional Services) and a healthcare trust specialising in the care of young people (Childcare Trust).

Software is a non-union company established nearly 20 years ago, which acquired two other companies in the last three years, giving rise to a need for organisational restructuring and moves to improve the integration of the three regional offices and Head Office. Around 280 staff are employed, 90 per cent of them software

professionals working in flexible teams with project-management responsibilities. An HR manager was appointed for the first time two years ago. Her view is that the workforce is neutral as between conflictual and consensual attitudes. She believes it is in the company's interest to take a positive approach to establishing consultative arrangements and has begun to consider what needs to be done in the light of the impending legislation. It is less clear that the directors understand the implications of the legislation or necessarily agree with a proactive approach.

Apart from legislative compliance, which is certainly one driver of the decision, there is a strong practical reason for taking the initiative. Bringing together three firms with different work practices and cultures presents an integration problem: many employees still seeing themselves as working for their former employer. The recent re-organisation was designed to deal with this by having functional groups of staff (such as development teams) all reporting to a single manager, irrespective of location. Although integration still remains elusive, staff had welcomed an *ad hoc* consultation set in motion by the MD to obtain employee opinion on how to capture better integration. This could well provide a favourable platform of recent experience on which to build.

As yet, the key design features are only loosely formulated. Table 4 on page 20 provides a checklist of questions being addressed alongside current thinking on the design issues. It is clear there is still much detail to be clarified, and that some significant policy issues for the company are involved: particularly whether rotation of directors in attendance would be better than a regular 'champion' able to provide some assurance of continuity and consistency to staff; and what

Table 4 | Key questions and initial throughts in a zero base firm

Key questions	Initial thoughts
Is there to be a single company consultative group?	*Probably yes, since relatively small company with some geographical spread.*
How many employee reps?	*Probably 6–10.*
How will the employee reps be obtained?	*Not yet considered.*
Who will be the management reps?	*One director attending each meeting on rotation.*
How often will it meet?	*2–4 meetings a year.*
Social aspects, given different locations?	*Desirable to establish some sense of common purpose, through social activity.*
What training provision, for whom?	*Lack of representative experience means training is desirable: training provided from outside the firm should be based on a good understanding of the firm and its objectives. Managers might also need training.*
What does the company want from this innovation?	*Just compliance or some positive purpose beyond this – if so, what? Sees consultation as an end in itself at the start, maybe able to move beyond this later.*
How can it convey this to participants?	*Not fully considered, but recognising importance of mutual understanding between the parties.*
What typical agenda items?	*Not clear, except issues arising from the re-organisation at the outset.*
What approach to consultation?	*Most likely to be of the reciprocal type – but that needs to be established and understood by the employee reps.*
What provision for reps to meet or prepare for meetings?	*Not yet considered.*
What is policy and procedure on disseminating outcomes?	*For consideration – could be electronic posting of minutes or decisions.*

objectives the company wishes to achieve through consultation in the longer term.

Professional Services has some 225 staff in total, including 28 partners and 72 fee earners. It has three main geographical locations, is a non-union organisation and has no history of institutionalised, information disclosure and consultation arrangements of either a direct or representative nature. The 'zero base' notwithstanding, the HR Director was keen to have arrangements in place before April 2005, with the following key target dates having been set:

- May 2004: the first team-brief in the organisation.

- September 2004: the election of employee representatives.

- December 2004: representative consultation body has its first meeting.

The case for these initiatives was made in a memo from the HR Director to the (seven-person) Policy Committee of the firm in the following manner:

Many organisations will sit tight and hope that their employees don't exercise these new rights. This is not a recommended option for us. We have already made a commitment to improving internal communication. It is the key to achieving more 'buy-in', increased motivation, better team working, a more consistent, positive culture and a resulting improvement in the bottom line. We have an opportunity to put in place a voluntary agreement on I&C, which will be an important tool in helping us to attain business objectives.

If we fail to use the next year to implement a positive, voluntary arrangement, we are likely to

have to spend time and money at a later stage, primarily to 'buy' compliance and with no guarantee that it will enhance our business objectives. We have already taken a positive first step by commissioning our recent report on internal employee communications. This demonstrates that there is an appetite for more communications and a willingness to contribute among those questioned.

The major findings of the report on internal employee communications referred to above were as follows:

Key findings of internal employee communications study

- The external consultant met with approximately 10 percent of employees, covering different locations, teams and roles.

- Staff were overwhelmingly positive about the firm as a place to work, and optimistic about their future.

- There was a perceived lack of communication about how well the firm was currently performing. There was also a lack of clarity and information about the firm's medium and longer-term goals.

- Meetings were solely department based, with their frequency varying a great deal between departments.

- Employees consistently indicated their desire to suggest ideas for improvement within the organisation.

> **'...the consultant recommended the introduction of team-briefing arrangements to handle information disclosure...'**

On the basis of these findings the consultant recommended the introduction of team-briefing arrangements to handle information disclosure, and subsequently, the creation of a standing body for elected employee representatives for dealing with consultation matters. The thinking behind this recommendation, which has been adopted by the firm, is that the very different processes of information disclosure and consultation require two different sets of arrangements, that disclosure must reach all the workforce directly, and that disclosure arrangements will be easier to set up first, thus providing a 'quick win' which can be built on by consultation.

Our third start-up case is Childcare Trust, one of our earlier case studies, which actually launched a consultative process a year ago, but it provides a useful guide to some of the issues that may arise when starting from a zero base. This organisation has a workforce of around 650, of whom 200 are casual staff. Employment is roughly 80 per cent female and widely dispersed throughout Scotland. A majority of staff are project staff, engaged on different programmes for young people in care. The Trust has been keen for some time to develop a representative consultative mechanism, and steps were taken to establish a consultative committee of nine representatives who would provide a cross-section of staff groupings and locations. Meetings would be quarterly, rotating among locations, in addition to a meeting with trustees and an annual staff conference with a specific thematic focus. This programme was superimposed on existing layers of management–staff dialogue as follows:

◻ continuous individual appraisal through the supervisor,

◻ weekly staff meetings dealing with local issues,

◻ sector group meetings enabling discussion on sectoral rather than organisation-wide issues, with management and Head Office involvement and feedback.

In the first phase of our research, it was proving difficult to obtain sufficient representatives and this problem has persisted, despite encouragement, regular reminders and time off allowed for representative duties. A maximum of six representatives has been achieved but at the second visit two employees had left employment, leaving only four representatives. Despite this, the participants feel that good progress has been made in the first year. The content of consultation covered a variety of issues eg pensions, pay and grading issues, voluntary organisation issues, IT, recruitment/retention, bullying and harassment, induction and appraisal.

Agenda items were initially suggested by management, mainly in our 'reciprocal' category (see Table 1 in Chapter 1, p10) derived from the HR department's planning priorities, covering external issues (eg legislation), social care practice and internal management issues. However, this fairly quickly moved to a more problem-solving approach dealing with issues that are just around the corner. In these cases, items are carried forward from one meeting to another, rather than being one-off discussions.

Consultation is envisaged mainly as a means to finding shared solutions, which is very much part of the social work culture and practice. Also, although agenda items prompted by staff tended initially to be individual issues, staff contributions to a wider agenda have started to emerge. The consultative committee also participated in implementing the closure of some services. The overall perception is that representatives are

> **'…many organisations had been prompted by the prospect of new legislation to re-examine their current practice, partly to ensure compliance would be satisfied but partly also to evaluate their experience with the existing model.'**

moving from people representing themselves to representation on behalf of the wider organisation. While there is much here that is encouraging, there is still a problem of failure to achieve a sufficient number of representatives, which may be due to a combination of staff structure, commitment to local rather than organisational priorities and the presence of effective alternative means of employee voice.

Developments of existing practice

Not surprisingly, we found many organisations had been prompted by the prospect of new legislation to re-examine their current practice, partly to ensure compliance would be satisfied but partly also to evaluate their experience with the existing model. In several cases, the review process highlighted areas that might be improved.

In Electronics, a non-union manufacturing establishment (one of our continuing cases), the elected members' council was centrally involved in dealing with the first ever compulsory collective redundancy in the organisation about three years ago, which involved one in three of the workforce losing their jobs. After all the drama, tension and hard decisions that were involved then, the meetings of the members' council had, at least in the view of the senior HR person, 'become little more than question and answer sessions', ie, the six elected employee representatives held prior meetings with their constituents, received a list of questions about a variety of matters and then passed these questions on for answer to the two management representatives in the council meetings.

In response to his view that the current process was 'a very tired one' the HR manager arranged for an external facilitator to work with the council

at one of their meetings to see to what extent his view was shared, and whether there was an agreed basis on which to move forward. A special full-day meeting of the council then followed this facilitated session at the end of which it was agreed to introduce the following changes in the mode of operation of the Council:

1   The name of the body was changed.

2   The chairing of the meeting would change at each meeting.

3   Each meeting would consist of two sizeable agenda items. The previous meeting would choose these, and within the meeting they will be referred to two sub-groups (each comprising three employee representatives and one management representative).

4   The two working groups would actively work to progress their items between meetings, with paid time off for this being given to the employee representatives.

5   The aim was to develop a joint problem-solving orientation where the following outcomes could occur: (a) the senior HR person (on the body) could make a decision; (b) the matter could be referred to the plant MD for a decision at an appropriate stage; or (c) more discussion, information and deliberation would take place within an agreed time frame.

6   Beyond these two core agenda items a small element of question and answer would be retained in each meeting.

7   Rather than the minutes of the body being emailed to all employees and placed on bulletin boards, the topics being addressed and the

'**The main aim is to deliver a consultative mechanism that will contribute to the strategic interests of the business for the benefit of the corporation and staff.'**

outcomes or state of progress would be included in the monthly business briefing provided by senior management to all employees, and a dedicated quarterly newsletter is being contemplated.

To help support these changes the employee representatives have agreed to raise many of their traditional questions with line management, seeking a relatively speedy decision; any difficulties in this regard are to be reported to the senior HR person. Furthermore, training sessions on both assertiveness skills and group facilitation skills have already been provided by an external trainer to all members of the new body, with the representatives being asked to identify any other perceived training needs. At the time of our most recent visit the HR Director was contemplating further training possibilities to help provide the representatives with more skills and self confidence to enable them to play a more proactive, 'leadership' type role in relation to the rapidly changing business needs of the facility.

IT Services, again one of our earlier cases, is a major global player providing IT and business process outsourcing facilities. It employs about 17,000 staff and recognises six unions, mainly PCS, which organises around 25 per cent of the UK workforce. There is a well-established European Works Council (EWC) in existence, but no formal collective consultation arrangements exist for the UK organisation other than for Health and Safety. The EWC has 29 employee representatives from a range of countries, four from the UK. Although experience with the EWC has been generally satisfactory, senior management would prefer it to be less formal and more purposive in its discussions.

Non-collective information and consultation is provided through an open door policy, supported

by employee messaging boards, 'town hall' talks and visits by company leaders. There is, however, no national (UK) consultative machinery, and the new legislation prompted the company to consider the advantages of a UK model, which might serve to address specifically UK issues, complementing the agenda of the EWC.

Two models were considered: one would have a single national body, the other as many as four bodies differentiated according to business function (the distribution is quite complex, reflecting the structure of the business organisation.) A preference emerged for the 4-forum model, on the grounds that as business leaders will have more ownership it will be more meaningful to staff and more likely to have a positive influence on the business because of its business function orientation. The single national body, in contrast, ran the risk that it would become a talking shop, doing little for the staff and contributing nothing to the business.

The model now proposed is for four bodies differentiated according to business area. The main aim is to deliver a consultative mechanism that will contribute to the strategic interests of the business for the benefit of the corporation and staff. However, it is recognized that 'reciprocal' consultation might at times be challenging because the corporate reporting structure cuts across national boundaries, and the locus of decision-taking in some cases lies outside the UK: this will not be simplified under the 4-forum model.

Soft Drinks, part of a global business, is concerned with the production, distribution and customer marketing of soft drinks. It employs 5,000 staff in 23 UK locations, with a 50/50 split between manufacturing and distribution/commercial activities. Union organisation is fairly strong

> **'These...cases indicate something of the variety of motivations for a relatively radical review of existing practice.'**

among operatives: just under 30 per cent of employees are covered by collective bargaining. An EWC has existed for several years, but British representation (in the absence of a UK representative structure) is not elected and not representative of the full workforce: the UK component exists in the form of a Forum of ten members, meeting twice a year, but not dealing with UK issues.

Following a strategic review about four years ago, a more integrative business strategy was adopted, with a stronger emphasis on people management. Employee surveys at that time revealed that the workforce positively wanted to be more involved and to have their opinions count (the prevailing production regime depends on highly standardised, uniform processes). Staff felt they had the ability to contribute, but their input was stifled: Management accepted this, took the view that higher engagement would lead to higher productivity, and that impending legislation would provide an opportunity to develop this.

Hence this was built into the strategy, on which detailed work has been ongoing now for 18 months. Although some UK business units had consultation arrangements in the form of works councils, they were uneven and incomplete, characterised as 'a patchwork', with some operating only as 'good news' bodies, not capable of handling more difficult issues, and lacking proper breadth of membership.

Ideally, it would have been better to build up from a business unit or local base of consultative groups, from which the national group would be elected. But in the absence of this, after consideration of other large-company models, the preferred model will aim at 20 employee members from three constituencies with seats proportional

to employment. They will be joined by four 'permanent' senior managers at VP level who will be in a position to contribute to most issues, while the proportional employee membership will avoid the dominance of manufacturing present in the EWC. Around 70 employees have put themselves forward for election – this will include some current members of the existing Forum.

The Group will meet at least twice a year, probably more at the start, depending on the agenda. The aim will be generally to provide information, consultation with a view to agreement, on a range of issues drawn from several sources, including the EWC – such as terms and conditions of employment, policy issues, changes in contractual relations – but not pay itself, which remains subject to negotiation.

These three cases indicate something of the variety of motivations for a relatively radical review of existing practice. In two of the cases, some unease or dissatisfaction with current EWC arrangements was a principal driver of change. The prospect of a new national UK structure provided the opportunity to rectify some of the existing design features, while establishing a mechanism appropriate to the company's UK requirements. It is significant, too, that a key aspect of these reviews was the desire on the part of management to ensure a closer fit between the consultative mechanism and the business needs, discussed further in Chapter 4. While this may not be a top priority from the point of view of employees and their representatives, it is clearly a legitimate concern from the managerial standpoint which seems quite consistent with the objectives of achieving more 'high performance workplaces' as envisaged in the DTI Consultation papers (DTI, 2002, 2003). The first of these examples also suggests an option for companies that are

> **'A further motive for amendment to existing practice is the relatively common problem of incorporating non-union employees into the consultative process, as the legislation requires.'**

dissatisfied with the performance of existing consultation arrangements and wish to revitalise them – in this case through a reconstruction of the underlying processes.

A further motive for amendment to existing practice is the relatively common problem of incorporating non-union employees into the consultative process, as the legislation requires. This is discussed in the following section.

Getting representatives

As we have seen in the Childcare Trust example, there may be organisations where it is difficult to obtain representatives, but this may be fairly unusual. The more common issues are likely to be those relating to generating an appropriate set of representatives who will be able to represent effectively the concerns and interests of their current workforce. The draft Regulations (2004) lay down quite clearly the conditions that will trigger proposals for an Information and Consultation agreement, the steps that have then to be taken for election of representatives and for ratification of the agreement. However, there is considerable scope for variation in the structure and representation arrangements for any organisation, and to a large extent the employer can shape this, for example in terms of a single ballot or separate ballots in different constituencies, provided that these proposals are agreeable to the representatives (if they exist) or the employees. (For further detail see Schedule 2 of the draft Regulations 2004).

In general, the Regulations appear to leave the organisation of representation to the parties to agree, provided only that the principles of fairness and openness in the ballot procedures laid down in Schedule 2 are followed.

Many existing arrangements, though otherwise satisfactory, involve only representatives of union members, reflecting the traditional approach to joint consultation as a parallel course to collective bargaining. The legislation, however, requires *all* employees to be covered by the arrangements and companies have had to re-think their approach. One of the most striking solutions to a large-scale problem of this sort has been seen in Telecom, a major telecommunications and IT services organisation, where the first level of 60,000 employees is 90 per cent unionised, and the next level of 30,000 about 60 per cent unionised, but leaving a further 14,000 staff at higher levels without union recognition. The solution was to extend full bargaining rights to about 7,000 sales staff through one of the existing unions, and to provide consultation rights to a further 7,000 staff, mainly management. Thus recognition now extends to all but about the top 1,000 managers, who would be principal decision takers themselves.

A more usual means of tackling this issue is likely to be found by providing for some form of representation from the non-union employees and providing them with the same information and consultation rights as the union representatives. Some unions may well have an antipathy to sharing consultation arrangements with non-union representatives, which would imply a dual channel, duplicating management input to the process.

This route has however been chosen by TV Co, which has recently experienced a significant merger, followed by post-merger rationalisation and some job losses. Union members totalled just under 1,000, but collective bargaining coverage was about 3,000. The other business in the merger had only partial union recognition. TV Co had previously taken the Article 13 route to employee representation, with elected representatives who

> **'A clear message from several of our cases with prior experience of consultation was that the new arrangements should be capable of making a distinct contribution to the business purposes of the organisation.'**

might be union or non-union. This provided a 'standing army' for consultation, to be used when needed.

This format is being applied to the merged organisation, adopting a form of twin-track consultation, comprising:

◘ consultative committees, all elected members, who may be union or non-union. There are around thirty such committees, with an average of 10 reps, hence a total of 300 representatives for 7,000 employees. Each has its own constitution, though they generally follow a common structure, worked out by each committee after initial training.

◘ union channels in areas where there is recognition: the aim, however, is to give prominence to the stewards, rather than national officers, as workplace representatives.

Determining the agenda and establishing expectations

A clear message from several of our cases with prior experience of consultation was that the new arrangements should be capable of making a distinct contribution to the business purposes of the organisation. If we consider the management of any organisation contemplating the establishment of a new or revised set of joint consultation arrangements, what lessons or insights could they draw upon from UK experience?

First, on the basis of a longer historical perspective, they would realise that voluntary, joint consultation arrangements have always played 'second fiddle' to the role of collective bargaining. This is reflected in the fact that joint consultative committees were not all that widespread, many

did not stand the test of time, and many had a relatively loosely connected agenda of numerous, but rather trivial (relative to collective bargaining coverage) items.

Second, they would note that in the relatively few statutory-based cases of joint consultation in the UK (eg collective redundancies, TUPE transfer) the process was conducted under very tight deadlines in which strong emotions and time pressures were present due to the 'crisis' nature of the problem they were seeking to deal with (eg proposed plant closure and subsequent job loss). On the basis of this experience, it is likely that the management of an organisation might seek to establish a joint consultation process that was in the middle ground between the two extremes of dealing with a one-off crisis event or having a very routine agenda of rather loosely connected 'small beer' items.

Equally clearly, our zero base cases suggested that while some had thought carefully about the agenda, others had not done so, a course which carries a strong risk that the new arrangements will quickly become trivialised and a source of irritation. Underlying this is a need for the parties to information and consultation to have a shared understanding of what the processes are about, what the aspirations are on both sides, and by implication, some general agreement on the sort of agenda items likely to feature prominently in the new framework.

Thus, in terms of cases already considered, Professional had been led to distinguish between provision for information disclosure and the setting up of a consultative committee, while Electronics had placed considerable emphasis on the desirability of moving consultation into the middle ground between the occasional crisis event and the routine of fairly trivial agenda items.

The agenda for consultation is not, of course, a prerogative of management. There has to be agreement between the parties as to what is expected of consultation and how the ground rules will be developed. In our earlier work we emphasised the importance of 'consultation about consultation', enabling the representatives to develop a clearer and mutually acceptable understanding of consultation as process. As a starting point one can obtain some useful, initial guidance from existing legal judgements concerning the notion of 'fair consultation' (Sargeant, 2001, p356) which has been viewed as having four basic pillars:

1   consultation should occur when management proposals are still at a *formative* stage.

2   management should provide *adequate* information as a basis for an informed employee response

3   there is an *adequate* time for the employee representatives to respond, and

4   management must demonstrate a *conscientious consideration* of the employee representative response.

The words in italics are key words, which the management and employee representatives need to focus on, flesh out in more detail, and then stick to in their consultation process. Two illustrative examples of how one might approach the task of providing the detailed content of these key terms are presented below.

Public Sector No.1 (a new case focusing on a large public sector organisation) has long had a joint negotiating body, which also incorporates the function of joint consultation. In practice the union representatives on this body have come from one union. This fact has become of increased concern to management as non-union employee numbers have grown in recent years. In response to a request from both the unions and management we conducted a set of five focus group exercises with groups ranging from senior managers to shop stewards with a view to seeing whether any consensus existed around the principles and practices of 'good effective consultation'. The leading results obtained are detailed below.

Perceptions of the principles of 'good, effective consultation'

The common themes which emerged from our five focus groups were as follows:

1   It is easier to say what consultation is *not*:

   ◘   a right of veto,
   ◘   a one way process,
   ◘   information disclosure.

2   *Strongest emphasis*: formal consultation processes will mirror the quality of the larger employee (union)–management relationship.

3   *Major errors to avoid*

   ◘   Unclear scope or coverage (Do we all agree just exactly what we are consulting about?).
   ◘   Management provides no rationale for the decisions ultimately arrived at.

4 *Value of the process*

It should generate additional options (beyond management's original list), which should then be narrowed down over time to result in a quality of final decisions that offsets the slowing-down of the decision-making process that must inevitably accompany consultation.

All focus groups agreed that this was not, however, the way the process was actually operating in practice and that changes needed to be made. Ideally the material obtained from the focus groups was to be utilised by a joint working party, which would further develop and refine in more detail the material outlined above. Unfortunately, this follow-up stage has not, as yet, taken place.

As indicated in our earlier report, DrinksCo (which now consists of a single business unit) had two prime-related objectives:

1 To produce a smaller, more cohesive EWC with a very focused Pan-European agenda.

2 To produce a UK-wide set of information disclosure and consultation arrangements which met its business needs, was in place before the first implementation due date, and whose membership represented the recent changes in the composition of the workforce; specifically, the growth in non-union employee numbers. The latter was perceived to be a particular challenge given:

◘ the strength of union representation in some parts of the organisation,

◘ the absence of any prior history of, or experience with, non-union employee representation.

Our case study research was primarily concerned with objective 2 above, although it is important to record briefly the fact that the objective of producing a smaller-sized EWC was achieved in practice. The UK-wide arrangements involved a total of 21 employee representatives, comprising three full-time officers and 18 elected representatives for nine functionally-based constituencies: the 18 representatives involve nine union and nine non-union employees. This body is scheduled to meet twice per year, these meetings being linked to the half-year and full-year reports of the organisation. However, special *ad hoc* meetings can be set up if requested on a perceived needs basis.

Throughout 2004 the body met on a number of occasions to agree the full details of its constitution, clarify its working relationship (eg representative numbers) with the new EWC, identify training needs and establish its working arrangements. In relation to the latter one of the earliest meetings extensively discussed the inter-related issues of training for representatives, communications with constituents and the nature of the consultation process. These discussions combined with training produced considerable elaboration and development of the process of consultation. In essence, the following three-stage process occurred:

1 Management sought to locate consultation in their larger 'philosophy' of organisational decision-making, and provided their list of what consultation is and is not.

2 An external body provided a training session for the employee and union representatives in

which the nature of the consultation process was central to the material provided.

3   Management representatives accepted the need to incorporate into the process the recommendations of employee representatives based on this training.

This process to date can be summarised as follows:

Developing and defining the process of consultation

1   Management presentation to newly elected employee representatives

- *Decisions will be taken by those best qualified to take them and influenced by those most affected by them.*
  (Overall view of decision-making).
- Consultation is *not*: decision-making or negotiating; telling; local or individual issues and grievances; delegates from workgroups; running a business area; bureaucratic, fixed.
- Consultation *is*: influencing decisions/taking views; two-way; good news/bad news; representative of business area; understanding business; flexible and responsible; evolving; confidential in part.

2   The key sessions/topics in the initial training programme were understanding and developing the role of the representative body, defining

consultation and developing a consultation strategy. Group work was extensively utilised and from the latter session emerged the recommendations listed below.

3   Management should:

- Adhere to the constitution by informing at the earliest opportunity.
- Give reasons for planned actions. This should include background on the market place, business goals, impact on the employees, impact on the business, and timescales.
- Listen to and respond to the representatives' feedback.

In response to the employee representatives' views a schedule has been added to the constitution of the body which, is as follows:

Consultation will normally take the following form; the company will share information and data with the council and allow members to acquaint themselves, examine and study that information as part of their preparation for consultation. The company will give the information and data in a form that can be readily understood. Where the information or data is particularly complex, expert advice may be sought in accordance with clause [...] of the Constitution. Council members will formulate views and opinions on the proposal and will be given the opportunity to explain these views and opinions at meetings. Where views and opinions are expressed, the company will provide a full response.

'**These examples underline the importance of going beyond the bare bones of a legalistic definition, however important that may be in terms of ensuring compliance.**'

In our judgement, this particular organisation made a considerable genuine effort to establish jointly an explicit set of ground rules for the process of consultation. However, whether such a 'good start' will automatically translate into a smooth, unproblematic process in action is a theme we return to in a later chapter when we revisit this particular case.

These examples underline the importance of going beyond the bare bones of a legalistic definition, however important that may be in terms of ensuring compliance. The case evidence indicates that misunderstandings – both on what consultation is and is not – are highly probable if they are not addressed early in the process. Without that fuller understanding, even though business can proceed for some time without real problems, there is a high risk that on a really important issue, the confusions will unravel, endangering the build-up of trust. This is discussed in detail in Chapter 4.

At a 'housekeeping' level, it is helpful to have understandings about the ground rules, with some forethought being given to the distribution of papers for the meeting, opportunity for exchanges of information within the parties, and possibly the 'social' interaction parallel to the business interaction. Thus in the case of the Childcare Trust, management meet briefly before meetings to ensure there is a shared understanding among them, though this is an open process in which employee representatives may participate. These representatives, who are geographically separated, can use the phone and own intranet for exchanges of views. (An employee representative confirmed that there is regular day-to-day contact on issues.)

Papers for the meeting are sent out well in advance, and representatives can get clarification on any point. The committee congregates the night before the meeting, where possible, to ensure it is 'seen as a process, not an event'. The business agenda and minutes are formal, otherwise the proceedings are informal and open, and representatives can ask for feedback.

Dissemination and actions

The final aspect of the initial list of set-up or review considerations relates to the dissemination of information about the work of the consultative committee and, equally important, ensuring that actions required in the aftermath of a consultation event are properly carried out by those responsible for taking matters forward. Here again, it is unwise to be prescriptive, since different organisations will have their own preferred means of conveying information, and what suits one organisation may be inappropriate in another.

The conventional means of informing employees abut the outcomes of consultation processes is probably the posting of formal minutes on a staff notice board, and the expectation that the employee representatives will pass on their account of events to their constituents. The risks of leaving it there are evident. Many staff will not read the notice board, and representatives may not give an entirely objective account of proceedings to their electorate. If the consultation process is dealing with significant issues, as one would hope, it is important that staff are given information about discussion without undue delay and if possible in terms that are agreed by the parties.

Companies are increasingly using intranet facilities to convey outcomes to all employees and while there is still no guarantee that all will read them, at least the opportunity to do so is equally provided. This may be particularly useful in organisations

> **'...this is what provides the challenge. There is no ready-made formula that can be acquired and applied with an expectation of success.'**

with employees distributed across a range of locations and activities. Just as important is the need to ensure that line managers are actively kept in touch with consultation developments: otherwise, the consultation process may seem to be working in a vacuum, and line managers may be left in the dark on how particular issues are shaping up. Equally, it is important that expectations of action being taken in the aftermath of a consultation are not frustrated, implying a real accountability on the part of those charged with taking agreed steps or engaging in further exploration of an item. Agreement on the degree of confidentiality necessary is often also important during certain discussions.

Concluding comments

This chapter has sought to highlight a range of approaches both to the setting up of consultation and information procedures from a zero base and to the review and development of established arrangements. Some of the issues arising are fairly self-evident, others less so, particularly perhaps in cases where organisations are moving forward simply to ensure compliance with the new legislative requirements. Our own reading of the evidence from our case studies is that the steps we have outlined are essential if the aim is to achieve an effective consultative and information infrastructure that will have a positive pay-off to both the employer and the employees.

The variety of circumstances we have encountered is certainly only a partial sample of the wide range of organisational intentions and characteristics, underlining the importance of recognising that there is no 'one size fits all' solution. But in a sense, this is what provides the challenge. There is no ready-made formula that can be acquired and applied with an expectation of success. What is needed is that organisations should seriously engage in self-analysis and appraisal, to ensure that they are clear about what they want to achieve, and that the employees and their representatives have an equally clear understanding of what is involved in *their* particular case. Employers should be interested more in best fit than in best practice. The listing of issues provided here should go some way to providing an agenda for such organisations to consider as they review their position. Our next step is to explore further some of the key factors likely to affect the degree of success they achieve.

4 | Key factors shaping the process of consultation

Introduction

In Chapter 2 we set out our analytic framework of the major determinants of the process of consultation, which comprised four elements: the context; the nature of the substantive issues; the values and expectations of the parties; and the stages of the process. In this chapter, we want to reflect some of the key factors that emerge from our cases, as viewed by the practitioners (both employer and employee). This involves taking a cross-cut on the previous analysis to focus on issues that appear to lie at the heart of the consultative process and determine its success. These issues relate to:

- The nature of the business being transacted in consultation.

- The role of representatives.

- Trust relationships.

- As a corollary, the preparation and training of representatives for the consultative role.

We treat each of these as a separate theme.

Theme 1: the nature of the consultative business

The historical evidence on joint consultation suggests strongly that the business being transacted in consultation has an enormous influence on the way consultation is viewed by the participants. We noted in Chapter 2 that there is a wide range of subject matter for joint consultation committees, but in practice there has been a considerable change in content. Marchington (1989) identified four models of consultation existing in Britain at the end of the 1980s:

- as an alternative to collective bargaining, to promote acceptance of managerial decisions;

- as a marginal activity, little valued by either management or employees, reflecting an absence of trust;

- as a competitor to collective bargaining, making the subject matter more significant and of vital interest to employees – with the implication that collective bargaining should be less important and

- as an adjunct to collective bargaining, with more openness of information and mutual recognition of employer and employee interests.

Perhaps the greatest change has been the transition from joint consultation perceived as a key element of *industrial relations* practice to consultation as an expression of employee voice within a *human resource management* paradigm, capable of building commitment in the workforce and contributing directly to the business's strategic aims of competitiveness and performance. Much more emphasis is placed on the output side of the equation, largely reflected in the American literature in the work of Kochan (1995) and Huselid (1995), but also in Britain by Guest and Hoque (1996) and Wood (1995), among others.

While there are some significant gaps in the postulated line of causation from employee voice to performance gains (Beardwell, 1998) there is little doubt that a low-level routine agenda with little direct relevance to the business interests is unlikely to develop mutuality, trust, commitment or business performance. In Chapter 3, we noted that, particularly within the larger organisations, there was a firm intent to realign consultation in

'…there is a need for both parties to have a secure understanding of what consultation is, and is not, and what are the appropriate areas for a consultative agenda.'

such a way that it becomes more capable of generating commitment and performance.

Two different, but not mutually exclusive approaches can be identified:

◻ Seeking to harness consultation to address strategic issues likely to face the organisation on a confidential basis, before any announcement of plans and policies (such as changes in policy on recruitment or changes in working practice affecting employee flexibility). This approach is very much: 'This is what we are proposing, what are your views?'

◻ Using consultation as a means of resolving high profile, high impact areas of actual or potential dispute between management and employees.

In both instances, there is scope for a joint problem-solving form of consultative activity, which is undoubtedly an aspiration of many participants (though we uncovered very few cases where training in problem-solving techniques had actually been provided). As we shall illustrate later, both approaches may be highly time-consuming and intense, well removed from a quick *tour d'horizon* and much more likely to involve a distinctly non-linear process, with many twists and turns as the exploration evolves (see Chapter 5).

It is significant that the companies that have seriously evaluated what they want from consultation (and the parallel provision of relevant information) are very clear that they need to avoid low-level business, which will in their view simply generate a turn-off, both for employees and for managers. This is a process that may well need to be 'managed', for there is ample evidence from our case studies that employee representatives

who fail to get the solutions they want at a lower level of consultation will seek to escalate these to the higher and more strategic levels of the consultative process. That has also been a common attribute of European Works Councils.

Again, therefore, there is a need for both parties to have a secure understanding of what consultation is, and is not, and what are the appropriate areas for a consultative agenda. The related question, of how the role of representatives in the consultation process is conceived, is our second theme.

Theme 2: a joint problem-solving consultation process requires employee representatives exhibiting the attitudes and behaviour of leaders, not delegates

Apart from the obvious requirement that employee representatives should provide a reasonable and practical cross-section of employee opinion, which will depend on the electoral arrangements, there is a deeper area of concern among many managements, relating to the expectation of the role that will be played by the representatives.

Part of this role is straightforward. The employee representative will be expected to convey employee opinion to management, since that is the expectation of the electorate. Likewise, the employee representatives will be expected to provide feedback to their constituents, though constitutional provisions may also delineate alternative means of disseminating information and keeping employees and line managers in touch with developments on current issues.

Beyond this, however, there is a question about how far the employee representative can be expected to act as a delegate of employees in the sense that he or she is committed to a particular view or set of instructions, or as a representative who will exercise independent judgement on the matters being discussed, though still maintaining an overall responsibility for safeguarding employee interests. This role of independent judgment will be particularly important where the matters under consideration fall into the joint problem-solving category.

In Chapter 3 we reported on the Electronics case where the senior HR person was keen to move away from a highly routine approach to consultation ('question and answer sessions') to more of a joint problem-solving one. In his view, the major stumbling block to this move was the current pattern of behaviour of some of the existing employee representatives who were strongly committed to acting as delegates for their constituencies.

To try to assist the process of moving from a delegate to a more proactive leadership role, training has been the major route identified; to date this has involved the provision of material on assertiveness skills and group facilitation skills. The senior HR person has, however, recognised that this and other training may not be adequate to produce the sort of attitude and behaviour change on the part of some of the representatives which he feels is essential. Arguments along those lines are common in a number of our other cases.

To gain further insights into this matter we conducted a detailed interview with an experienced consultant who has worked closely with a sizeable number of employee representatives in consultation situations (eg collective redundancies, TUPE, and others). From this interview a clear view emerged on the

attitudes and behaviours which make for an 'effective' employee representative. In essence her opinion was as follows:

- An effective representative is able to clearly distinguish between their responsibilities as a representative and those responsibilities that follow from their employee role.

- They recognise very early on that such representative responsibilities will impose considerable pressure on them, which they are able to adjust to and cope with.

- In the early stages of acting as a representative they see their prime role as being the mechanism for conveying the employees' views of their circumstances and needs to the management.

- However, over time, as experience and confidence is gained, they tend to increasingly alternate between acting as a delegate or as a leader, depending on the needs and circumstances of the occasion. For example, their attitudes and behaviour changed according to whom they were speaking, and whether this involved open or closed sessions.

This interview highlighted three important things to us. First, experience, as well as training, will be important in shaping representatives' attitudes and behaviour. Second, representatives' attitudes and behaviour may need to change according to circumstances. Third, an effective employee representative has to juggle and balance responsibilities to two groups: their workforce constituents and the management representatives they deal with. This third point leads us into our next major theme, that of trust.

> **'We accept completely the important role of trust in the process of consultation, but feel that the term is all too often used in a rather vague and general way.'**

Theme 3: The notion of trust in the process of consultation involves multiple levels and multiple determinants

Throughout our case study visits and discussions with practitioners (both employees and management) we have typically heard contentions such as the following:

In the absence of trust, no set of consultation arrangements will work.

Or

If trust is undermined, the existing arrangements will achieve very little.

We accept completely the important role of trust in the process of consultation, but feel that the term is all too often used in a rather vague and general way. Specifically, we feel that there has been too little attention given to:

◘ The *focus* of the trust relationship (between whom does it need to exist?)

◘ Identifying the key *determinants* of trust, and the extent to which they are under the control of the representatives directly involved in the consultation process.

We would argue that in the context of the process of joint consultation trust needs to exist at all three of the following levels or points:

1   Between constituents and their representatives.

2   Between the representatives directly engaged in the consultation process.

3   Between the representatives and, what we term here, 'the larger organisational context'.

In this chapter, although all three levels of trust are important for the process of joint consultation, we particularly highlight the potential importance of level 3, for two main reasons.

First, in our experience it is from this level that damage to the operation of joint consultative arrangements so often derives in practice. Second, much of the academic work on trust has been done in the area of conflict resolution where a fairly standard definition of trust is as follows:

an individual's belief in, and willingness to act on the basis of, the words, actions and decisions of another.

(Lewicki, McAllister and Bies, 1998, p440)

Implicit in such a definition is that the trust relationship is overwhelmingly a function of (for good or bad) individuals that you directly deal with across the table.

In the context of joint consultation, we argue that such a perspective on trust is an important part of the story, but far from the full story. Indeed we would argue that level 3 above is of increasing importance in view of the fact that in the contemporary environment the organisational context in bigger firms is changing rapidly, and is also becoming increasingly complex in nature, such that the capacity to develop trust with particular individuals across the table is becoming more difficult. In short, we are emphasising an analogy to the distinction drawn by Alan Fox (1985) between vertical and horizontal trust.

> **'...the organisational context in bigger firms is changing rapidly, ...such that the capacity to develop trust with particular individuals across the table is becoming more difficult.'**

In our view it is useful to consider the level and nature of trust as being shaped by at least three important set of influences or factors:

1   The nature of the broader, historical relationship between employees (unions) and management ('historical baggage').

2   The degree of shared expectations and understanding between the employee (union) and management representatives across the table ('the ground rules') about how the process will, and should be, conducted. (This set of influences was, of course, the subject matter of Chapter 3.)

3   The degree of confidence the representatives (particularly on the employee side) have in the larger organisational context, particularly as this context changes and becomes more complex in nature.

These three sets of influences undoubtedly overlap to a very considerable extent. But we believe it is helpful to make such a distinction because it emphasises the potentially rather fragile nature of the joint consultation process, where positive trust relationships between the representatives across the table are important, but certainly no guarantee that the consultation process will remain viable and meaningful over time. That is, they can be shaped or disrupted at levels beyond the reach of the consulters.

Historical baggage

The way in which historical circumstances shape current perceptions and expectations of the 'value' and 'effectiveness' of contemporary joint consultation arrangements will vary substantially between different organisations. However, what does not seem to be in doubt is the fact that contemporary perceptions and expectations will be strongly shaped by historical experience. This may derive from previous experience with consultative arrangements, although even in organisations where there has been no prior consultative experience the absence of experience may be an important influence. Moreover, in all organisations, historically-based perceptions of the larger employee–management relationship will be influential (albeit in different ways) on current perceptions of the worth of current consultative arrangements.

To illustrate how no new (or reformed) contemporary consultative arrangements can start with a 'blank sheet' we will briefly discuss three of our recent cases which indicate very different 'starting' points in terms of current employee and management expectations. In the Electronics plant the members' council has been meeting monthly for the full life of the plant (over ten years). Only in the last year has the company established UK-wide joint consultative arrangements by setting up a body to meet on a quarterly basis including employee representatives from its two non-manufacturing sites.

Employee focus groups conducted in the two non-manufacturing sites overwhelmingly point to employee *uncertainty* regarding the potential value of the new consultative arrangements. Their responses indicated a limited understanding of the nature of the consultative process, and considerable doubt as to whether such a process could be of any real value to them as individuals or a group ('you will listen to us as representatives, but ultimately you can decide to ignore our views'). Further, there was concern that the

> '...a sizeable majority of respondents believed that "consultation has no effect because management has already made up its mind".'

agenda of the UK-wide body could ultimately be dominated by the agenda and experience of representatives from the relatively large manufacturing site. Interestingly no employee representative elections needed to be held in the two non-manufacturing sites as the number of employees who were nominated to be representatives did not exceed the number of representatives required.

In marked contrast is the perceived (by management) relatively *optimistic* starting point among staff in Professional Services. This organisation is planning for the first time to introduce team-briefing arrangements (for information disclosure purposes) and then employee representative arrangements based on their newly reorganised set of business units. As a background exercise they had an external consultant conduct a series of group interviews with approximately ten per cent of the workforce. This exercise revealed:

◘ a considerable lack of understanding among staff about the current performance and future business plans of the firm as a whole,

◘ a very considerable desire on the part of staff to actively contribute to the process of business improvement in the organisation.

It is the latter finding that management view as a relatively positive basis on which the new arrangements must seek to build.

Our third and final illustrative example in this section suggests that perceptions of the workforce, as shaped by historical experience (at least as they see it), suggest an essentially *cynical* attitude towards proposals for change in consultation arrangements. In Engineering, our

questionnaire responses and focus group material overwhelmingly revealed that a sizeable majority of respondents believed that 'consultation has no effect because management has already made up its mind'. On the basis of this material we would expect relatively limited numbers of nominations for people willing to act as representatives, and constituents who are not strongly behind their representatives in the sense of being actively and meaningfully engaged in the process.

Beyond the reputations and stereotypes emerging from historical experience (albeit perhaps selectively recalled), inter-personal experience, particularly over time, is important in shaping trust between the representatives around the consultation table. Typically, researchers (see for example Lewicki, and Wiethoff, 2000) have argued, at least in the context of conflict resolution, that creating trust in a relationship is:

1 initially a matter of building *calculus-based* trust (ensuring consistency of behaviour, with people doing what they say they will),

and then

2 moving on to the build up of *identification-based* trust where there is an increasingly shared identification with the 'other side's' aims and objectives.

Both the process of moving from 1 to 2 and the maintenance of 1 itself over time can be, as we illustrate below, subject to disruption from factors outside the control of the consulters.

Trust in the larger organisational context

Our research suggests that representatives engaged in consultation can, at least in principle, experience two different sorts of trust difficulties with the larger organisational context:

◘ 'Passive resistance' whereby their recommended options or views seem to get absorbed, lost or selectively interpreted at various rather vague decision points in the larger organisational hierarchy.

◘ The notion of a 'strategic shock' whereby a specific announcement or decision by senior management is held to be 'inconsistent' with the explicit or implicit ground rules of consultation, and indeed ultimately suggests the very limited reach and effectiveness of the consultation process.

In our experience these sorts of upsets to the consultation process have been particularly powerful when the process is embedded in larger partnership working arrangements (Beaumont and Hunter, 2003). Below are two cases designed to illustrate the above two lines of argument; the first case is an example of the former – ie passive resistance, with the second case being concerned with the latter, a strategic shock.

Passive resistance

This case study (Public Sector No. 2)[1] involves two key management themes in recent years, which are:

◘ The need to ensure that management decisions are not solely determined by supply-side interests, and hence the key importance of engaging in a wider stakeholder consultation process;

◘ The notion of joined-up government, which can be tangibly manifested in various ways,

such as the integration of service delivery across two independent organisations in order to reduce resource duplication and provide more effective delivery for end users.

These two lines of development have the potential to significantly reduce employee representative perceptions of the worth of any employee consultation process, and hence can seriously damage the viability of such a process over time. In essence, reported here are employee perceptions of a relatively positive process of interaction, but much more uncertainty and concerns over the likely outcome of their deliberations as their recommendations entered the larger organisational context. Hence the use of the earlier term 'passive resistance'.

The case study was located in the context of the Joint Futures Initiative that seeks increasingly integrated aspects of service delivery between providers in the health service and social work. Specifically we examined the activities of five working groups of occupational therapists (each comprising individuals from social work and health) who were given the task of producing a set of recommendations for change under certain specified terms of reference that would enhance the move to integrated service delivery. Their input represented one aspect of an extensive consultation process governed within the overall community care planning structure.

As background to our research work the following points should be noticed:

◘ Both health and social work have a long history of consultation with union representatives only, and this process was continuing alongside that of the working group deliberations.

> **'...we have done what we can but we are not sure how much will be taken on board.'**

◘ This was the first experience that the vast majority of the occupational therapists had of being involved in such a consultation process.

◘ Strictly speaking there were no management representatives on the working groups although all groups were facilitated by more senior people, one of whom was a member of the steering group for integrated services in occupational therapy.

◘ Alongside the five working groups were a variety of other joint future initiatives of a similar nature for other occupational groups.

Our research involved focus group discussions with all five working groups, together with the completion of short individual questionnaires by members of the groups. Both sets of information obtained (see Table 5, opposite) strongly pointed to very different views about the process of working together, and the outcomes of this working.

In summary, all five working groups appeared to gel relatively quickly, reported that they had enjoyed the process, had learned from it and were willing to repeat the process. However, there was a very important condition to their willingness to repeat the exercise, namely their concern as to how their recommendations would be received by, and responded to, in the larger organisational context. In this regard, both uncertainty and scepticism were very much in evidence. Issues raised by the group members included the relatively long time period between when they began their work (November 2003) and the earliest possible implementation date (April 2005) for any recommendations and the long, drawn-out consultation process involving other relevant stakeholders. Other concerns were over the lack of

knowledge of other working groups engaged in similar exercises, a belief that occupational therapy was not a high priority in the larger integration agenda; and above all, fears about the level of resources, funding and political and managerial will to underpin their recommendations. These all combined to produce the view that 'we have done what we can but we are not sure how much will be taken on board'.

A strategic shock

An example of this notion is provided by Engineering, one of our ongoing cases. This foreign-owned organisation has a number of facilities in the UK. In recent years UK management has in all of its facilities sought to establish partnership-type working arrangements in which the elements of consultation and trust are held to be absolutely central. However, a statement by an individual in corporate headquarters that a UK facility was to be closed, and the product transferred to a newly-built facility in another country, was reported in the news media, and quickly reached the ears of union officers, shop stewards and employee representatives in the UK.

They forcefully made the point to UK management that the fact that this information was in the public domain before they were aware of it was unacceptable for three major reasons:

◘ It suggested that management did not trust them as individuals.

◘ Any such announcement was inconsistent with the organisation's rhetoric concerning partnership consultation, trust etc.

◘ It suggested that consultation on the issues that really matter to employees (ie employment

Table 5 | Some key research findings from employee consultation

Employer – 59% Health Service (NHS); 41% Social Work Services (SWS). 50% having been in their current employment for more than 10 years.

Involvement in the consultation process was **voluntary** for **63%** of working group participants. The remaining 37% were nominees. **73%** had **not previously been involved** in a process of this nature. The employees' main perceived contribution to working groups was personal experience (see below). It is notable that only four participants had any managerial responsibility for implementation.

	Main contribution (count)*	Secondary contribution (count)*
Strategic knowledge about the service	7	5
Client group knowledge	6	11
Management responsibility for implementation	1	**3**
Extensive experience in clinical or social work practice	**15**	9
Experience of working in teams	6	7
Previous experience of service integration	2	2
Other (please specify)	3	1

*Number of employees

Perceptions of the working group

The extent to which the work groups perceived themselves as teams differed considerably, with **39%** viewing themselves as a **collection of individuals** rather than a coherent team. In contrast, **27%** described their working group as having a **shared bond and sense of identity**.

Although there was variance as to the extent to which they perceived themselves as a team, there did appear to be strong **identification with the team** (**75%** identified closely with their working group) and **high trust** (**97%** felt that there was a trust relationship between group members). Interestingly, **86%** felt their contribution to the group was of **personal importance**. This should be understood alongside the fact that **83%** agreed/strongly agreed that group contribution was important for **career development** purposes.

Illustrative quotes

▫ *...[we] mostly enjoyed [the process], found it educational, an eye opener, and found it reassuring to see we shared views on the OT role...*

▫ *...[I] felt the consultation and role in it was important but there's an element of symbolism in the process ...we have done what we can but we're not sure how much will be taken on board.*

security) are a complete waste of time, with the final decisions having already been reached in venues outside the reach of the consultation process.

To try and offset this damage, senior managers from corporate headquarters, in conjunction with UK management, have spent a great deal of time in making presentations in the UK, and indeed in other EU member countries, the essence of these being as follows:

- There has been something of an apology given in the sense of acknowledging a failure on the part of corporate headquarters to fully understand and appreciate all the details of this 'foreign' consultation process.

- A very detailed presentation of the business case that had been given to senior management and which provided the basis for the closure decision.

Beyond these short-term responses, corporate management has given the following commitments:

- In future, any facility experiencing cost, productivity, quality etc problems on a sufficient scale to raise question marks about its longer-term viability would be involved in a dialogue with headquarters which would make it clear just how much they had to improve performance, and by when in order to avoid such an outcome.

- Employee representatives, stewards and union officers in all UK facilities were invited to get together to produce an agreed list of best practice principles which they would wish to see embodied in the consultation process

where closures and sizeable job-loss were involved. This list of principles will then form the basis for discussions concerning their possible incorporation into company-wide business procedures for dealing with such situations. The input of one union to this ongoing exercise is summarised below.

A union view of principles for informing and consulting when restructuring

These are principles that would be applied when a plant closure or major restructuring is anticipated by the company.

- Employees have the right to learn of the loss of their job direct from the senior manager at the location or a more senior business leader and not from a source internal or external to the company.

- It is the company's responsibility to ensure that employees at a local entity level should understand the challenges arising from both cost and new products. Employees should be aware of what is required at their location for a sustainable business.

- The intent should be that if the Company proposed solutions that led to a job loss, employees might be concerned and angry but they should not be unaware of why it was happening.

- Should the Company believe that the need has arisen for restructuring they

'**...what we have here is an organisation beginning the process of trying to recover and rebuild some of the trust among employee representatives that was substantially shaken, not to say lost, by this particular "strategic shock".**'

will initiate a process of consultation as timely as possible recognising the need for confidentiality.

- ◘ The Company recognised that informed sharing of information with local senior employee representatives and the Chair of the consultative committee on behalf of all employees may be appropriate.

- ◘ The Company, where it is commercially feasible, will give a reasonable opportunity for employees to suggest alternatives to the business decision, which would remove the need for restructuring.

In short what we have here is an organisation beginning the process of trying to recover and rebuild some of the trust among employee representatives that was substantially shaken, not to say lost, by this particular 'strategic shock'.

Theme 4: training matters

To complete this chapter, we turn our attention to the implications for the training of representatives engaging in consultation. A number of practical considerations regarding training immediately come to mind:

- ◘ How important is training for effective representation in the consultation context?

- ◘ Is training necessary for managerial as well as employee representatives – and if so, should the training be provided jointly?

- ◘ Should the training be provided in-house or bought in from a consultant or training agency?

- ◘ What should be the main focus of training?

Importance

In general, our case evidence suggested that most organisations recognise the desirability of training for employee representatives, though by no means all had got round to making it available. It was significant, however, that where companies were involved in EWC arrangements, considerable effort was devoted to training representatives, suggesting that when consultation moves into a more formal and sustained mode, the investment in proper training is seen to be more essential.

Because a number of our cases were moving to a consultative mode for the first time, and others, though accustomed to consultation, were introducing new constituents (such as non-union employees) or new thinking into their consultation arrangements, we would expect that the demand for training for consultation will increase. New representatives are likely to have only a sketchy understanding of consultation activities and roles, and will need some form of preparation. Existing representatives will bring with them their own historical baggage, as we have seen above, and if a new start is to be made, training to acclimatise them to the change would obviously be desirable.

Joint management and employee training

In companies with well-established consultation, training has often been provided in the past, or even as an ongoing activity. The pattern we have commonly observed is that this training is provided

> **'This assumes that managers will already have the knowledge and skills appropriate to consultation, which is at least a debatable point.'**

for employee representatives alone. Companies may recognise that there is a need in the training context to align the thinking and attitudes of employee and management representatives, but the most common way of addressing this was to have some management staff contribute to the training by providing one or two sessions outlining the specific organisational approach and value system. This assumes that managers will already have the knowledge and skills appropriate to consultation, which is at least a debatable point. The thinking of TV Co in this respect, detailed below, is instructive:

Consultation is not a soft option

'Management has a strong belief in the value of consultation, but takes the view that *wording and tone are important*, and managers have been trained to speak in terms such as "the plan is to…" – then await reactions, giving time for consideration and response. In management training, an aim has been to develop better understanding of negotiation and consultation. *Initial responses from managers were that negotiation was "tough", while consultation was "soft" – but that view has now changed. Negotiation is easier because it follows rules and formal stages: consultation requires listening, taking issues on board, and learning. It is essential to build in time and space, allowing some areas to be unformed, before actions are taken. Management also needs to be alert against too early issue of press releases on matters such as site closures, and managers have*

---

been trained to avoid doing so. These points help to relieve the problem of challenges that consultation has taken place too late. While management wants to gain what it can from consultation for its own purposes, this is quite consistent with meeting employee expectations and aspirations. Lessons from consultation can often lead to opportunities to include changes or new items in the "plan".

Today's business is seen as depending increasingly on consultation, and listening time is time worth spending. Management has had to learn to consult and develop a sense of "respectful engagement".' (From case notes)

The inference here is that consultation skills and strategic awareness are not something that can be taken for granted. The constructive purpose of consultation may be lost or reduced if inappropriate attitudes and behaviours are brought to the process.

There is probably a good deal to be said for having at least some form of joint training activity to ensure that approaches are aligned – or where not, at least that the differences are brought out into the open. This might be achieved, for example, by having one or more 'away-day' joint sessions, where it is understood that this is not simply for the benefit of employee representatives but equally for the benefit of managers – putting them clearly on the same footing[2].

This is likely to be even more important where there is a serious intention to develop consultation into the joint problem-solving arena, where the

> **'Probably on grounds of expense, many organisations use in-house resources to provide employee training for consultation.'**

systematic selection and application of problem-solving tools needs to be shared openly and equally by all the participants, if success is to be achieved. (We encountered a number of organisations that said they engaged in problem-solving consultation but appeared not to have provided any training for this. It seems important to register the point that problem-solving approaches are not just a matter of a consultative group trying, somewhat randomly, to work out a solution, but really require a more rigorous and structured approach, which only proper training is likely to produce.)

In-house or externally-provided training?

Probably on grounds of expense, many organisations use in-house resources to provide employee training for consultation. This also serves the useful purpose of ensuring that the training provided is attuned to the specific plant or company context and culture, which will always be a necessary ingredient. However, training provided by an external facilitator is likely to be more objective, as viewed by the employee participants, who may in extreme circumstances, especially where there is a relative absence of trust, feel that they are being 'brain-washed'.

This may well be exaggerated when accompanied by short visits and addresses from senior managers, outlining the corporate approach. Thus although companies will almost certainly continue to use different methods, there is a good deal to be said for using some measure of external input, supplemented by appropriate and well-balanced internal contributions. Equally, it should be said that purely external provision has its own limitations if it does not fully integrate with the style and purpose of the client organisation. For this reason, some companies use training

consultants who already have experience of working with the firm and are well-briefed on its procedures and aspirations for consultation.

The focus of training

Some of the characteristics required of successful and effective consultation participants have been detailed on page 44. However, individual organisations will need to consider their own context and environment, and the role that they wish consultation to fulfil. In that respect, they should at least consider undertaking a form of training needs analysis (for the consultative purpose), which may pinpoint specific areas of concern or emphasis. These in turn can be used to brief either internal trainers or external training consultants.

An interesting example of just this sort of thinking emerged in one of our cases (Communications – to be considered more fully in Chapter 5). Table 6 on page 46 sets out a summary analysis of what consultation participants are currently revealing in the way of attitudes, behaviour and expectations, parallel to the future state to which the organisation aspires, which is much more a joint problem-solving approach. The skills and capabilities required are shown in column three, these are allocated into personal, behavioural and informational categories in column four and finally related back to consultative capabilities in the final column.

This is an impressive analysis (backed up by much more detail than is possible to provide here), demonstrating that for this sort of aspirational approach, starting from a relatively low level of achievement and expertise, there is an extensive and demanding training programme required. This, of course, could only be contemplated by a

'The provision of training...is likely to be a key differentiator between those organisations that recognise the long-term benefits of informing and consulting their workforce and those that are just going through the motions.'

Table 6 | Outline training needs analysis

'Now' State	'Future' state	Skill or capability needed	Category of need	Link to capability
Defers to negotiating style when trying to solve a business problem Resorts to registering disagreement via the IR framework	Knowledge of the joint problem-solving (JPS) toolkit Ability to undertake joint problem-solving	◘ Understanding of JPS toolkit ◘ Team-working ◘ Facilitation ◘ Information-gathering and research	Personal, informational	(detailed under headings: inspires people, seeks improvement, takes ownership)
Inability to consult and involve Low ability to evaluate options	Confident in asking for other opinions, weighing up input and making a decision Ability to do option-based consultation/ negotiation, capable of using GROW model	◘ Consultation – leading and participation ◘ Active listening ◘ Facilitation ◘ Behaviours ◘ Information-gathering and research ◘ Decision-making ◘ Leadership ◘ Team-working ◘ Understanding of planning and decision models	Personal, behavioural, informational	

well-resourced organisation, but the approach to, and content of this analysis may provide valuable clues for practitioners in other organisations.

Conclusions on training

The provision of training for employee representatives and management involved in information and consultation is likely to be a key differentiator between those organisations that recognise the long-term benefits of informing and consulting their workforce and those that are just going through the motions.

Both employee representatives and management need an understanding of the concepts, processes and mechanisms of information and consultation.

'Investment in training on information and consultation reveals to representatives and the workforce as a whole that the organisation is taking the issue seriously.'

Joint training for management and employee representatives can help improve mutual understanding and develop working relationships. Training is also important to help representatives learn to work together, particularly in cases where there are union and non-union representatives in the same consultative group.

Investment in training on information and consultation reveals to representatives and the workforce as a whole that the organisation is taking the issue seriously. The costs of failing to make this investment are potentially considerable, particularly given that there are a lot of generic skills needs that can be addressed relatively quickly.

Endnotes

1   We are most grateful to our colleagues, Moira Fischbacher and Judy Pate, for the major roles they placed in this particular study.

2   The major danger to guard against here is generating any adverse perceptions among employee constituents that the employee and management representatives may be 'getting too cosy'.

5 | The dynamics of consultation

In earlier chapters we have been mainly concerned to try to break down the process of consultation into a number of vignettes, allowing us to explore the detailed issues that arise in practice. However, to leave the matter there would be to miss one of the key characteristics of a great deal of consultation, which is that it will often have its own dynamic as it proceeds through a number of stages. In relatively routine matters, of course, this is less likely, but when major issues of serious importance to the parties are at stake, consultation may lead into unexpected areas of difficulty or opportunity which cannot be disposed of in a single session. In this chapter, therefore, we try to give some impression of the sorts of issues that may arise over time and the patience, perseverance and improvisation that may be required if a successful outcome to the process is to be achieved.

We present three cases, which illustrate this dynamic, and further illustrate how many of the issues we have already discussed come into play as the processes are played out. These issues include early disclosure of management intentions, the need for clear agendas that are mutually understood, the different skills deployed in consultation and negotiation and the possibility that consultation may lead on to negotiation.

In presenting these cases in a timeline form, we have taken the view that rather than leave our comments and interpretation to the end of the case, it is more helpful to insert commentary as the events unfold. This allows the main learning points to be noted at the stages of the process revealed by the narrative. Our commentary is identified by being printed in coloured italics. Each case is preceded by a brief synopsis of the features of the consultation arrangements.

Case 1: Telecom

Key features:

This very large employer has 90 per cent union membership distributed between a blue-collar and a white-collar union, and European Works Council is in place. Pay and conditions are negotiated at national (UK) level. There is no national JCC and no formal JCC structure, but there is a *de facto* national forum and a 'line of business' structure of ongoing consultation, which deals with problems of change and business-driven issues on a continuing basis. The intention is to continue with this model, which is issue-driven and often fused into bargaining – though not on pay matters. Depending on the issues, the discussion may be national, local or line of business, and meetings typically take place weekly – only separating formally to talk about pay issues. Consultation is viewed as having real value and a critical part of the union–management relationship – especially through the regular informal contact between the HR Director and full-time officers that enables early signalling of intention.

Business strategy as the trigger

A major plank in Telecom's business strategy, faced with a declining market in its traditional core business of telecommunications, is to extend its global reach, particularly in the area of combined communication/IT – a rapidly expanding market. As part of this strategic approach it formed an alliance with a major US IT company (Usco), to provide a multi-sourced solution to the convergence of communications and IT in the global market, providing a broader scope for serving the existing and new customer base. This aimed at a 3-stage development:

i   workstream 1: outsourcing (to Usco) Telecom's current mid-level IT work (a support desk and

'Consultation starts at any early stage while the details are still incomplete, in recognition of the sensitivity of the issues that will arise.'

managed service functions for customers). This involved the transfer of 300 staff to Usco (with a smaller reverse flow), which is protected by TUPE regulations, requiring consultation: also a further 300 staff not covered by TUPE, working as contract employees to Telecom. This is seen as a platform on which the later development can be built.

ii workstream 2: further plans for similar project to workstream 1

iii a joint take-to-market proposition for the new organisation providing an integrated service.

The focus here is on i above, but the other plans are relevant. Both parties saw the partnership solution as appropriate, using complementary strengths to penetrate the global market; and initial plans were made to a point where disclosure of intent was necessary at the end of 2003.

Timeline of process

Disclosure of intent started in December 2003, when the proposal was still covered by non-disclosure agreement between the parties. Confidential briefing on the broad lines of the proposition and its strategic rationale was given to senior officers of the two Telecom (blue-collar and white-collar) unions, with a probable timescale. This confidential consultation was carried out because of

1 the strategic significance of the project,

2 likely resistance from employees, given the seniority and age of those likely to be involved, and

3 resistance to outsourcing generally, as part of Telecom culture.

The aim at this stage was to identify the main resistance points for the unions.

The scene is set, with a change that is seen as central to future business strategy, which will affect a small but significant number of employees. Consultation starts at any early stage while the details are still incomplete, in recognition of the sensitivity of the issues that will arise.

The unions were opposed to the change: their instinct was that Telecom was 'selling the family silver'. They had concerns that the company would become a mere network provider (supplying a commodity market); that earlier projects had not been successful, and that the end could be achieved without transfer of employees – eg by secondment for a period. (This latter line remained an issue of lobbying and pressure through the duration of the consultation till the very end.)

The two companies developed the plan in more detail in the period January/February 2004, paralleled by meetings of the lead Telecom negotiator and the top blue-collar union official to clarify strategy and allay concerns – but issues remained. It was agreed that a senior Telecom manager would give a detailed presentation to senior union officers of both unions, covering market context, strategic value, market potential etc. The issue of union representation would also be covered, since Usco is a non-union firm.

Resistance to the change is confirmed, and an iterative process of informal contacts between the leading actors is begun. Steps are taken to provide systematic information in more detail to ensure that the rationale of the change is understood. The efforts to move the employee representatives to a more favourable position have begun.

March 2004: start of formal consultation

1 Management presentation to wider group of union officers – national officers and executive members of both union. It was agreed to aim for completion of the agreement in early May, within three months; it was also agreed how the consultation should be taken forward.

> **'Activity intensifies, involving an almost continuous dialogue between the parties at top level, but extending more widely.'**

2   This was followed three days later by Telecom providing a full briefing to affected employees, spread across different sites and business units, with a question and answer mechanism to respond to staff concerns.

Telecom gave assurances that the deal would be fair and reasonable for the transferred staff, and would involve a favourable contribution to pension arrangements and protect job security – but not the right of return to Telecom, which was not conceded.

The reaction from both union officers and staff consulted confirmed the following main issues:

◻ Maintenance of terms and conditions for affected staff: dealt with by systematic working through of matrix of terms for both organisations – able to reach agreement on this.

◻ Union representation of staff after transfer: informal meeting arranged with senior Usco managers agreed that transferred staff would get representation and bargaining rights within Usco.

◻ The big issues were *pension rights*, highly technical, for which a separate group was set up, and *job security*.

The information and consultation process begins to roll out to a wider audience, particularly those employees likely to be affected by the change. Timescales for completion of consultation leading to a consensus are established. The likely areas of contention are identified and confirmed from the initial wider soundings.

Pensions: a different TU lead negotiator had to be appointed for this issue – the main lead was a pensions Trustee and had a conflict of interests. The unions were adamant that there should be no loss of pension entitlement to those transferred: the aim was for actuarial equivalence. A series of meetings followed in sequence:

i   clarifying the formal positioning of the parties

ii   a follow-up in very frequent informal discussions with different individuals and groups, continuing a dialogue working towards agreement, testing and checking, refining.

iii   a series of pension seminars was provided for those affected, to answer specific questions about entitlement, etc.

iv   agreement in early May between management and senior union officers *at consultative level* on a scheme that would have employees make a four per cent contribution, relative to the employer's 12 per cent. As compared with Telecom's final salary scheme this had some advantages offset by higher risk, though some would gain. Where there was a shortfall in provision, Telecom offered to provide 'focused funding' to cover it.

Activity intensifies, involving an almost continuous dialogue between the parties at top level, but extending more widely. This is accompanied by more detailed briefing of affected employees on the way individual pension rights will be handled, seeking to increase understanding and relieve anxiety. To achieve this, Telecom recognises that a 'sweetener' is required to encourage progress towards agreement.

Job Security: The unions wanted a guarantee of no compulsory redundancy for the project's duration (seven years) and the right to return to Telecom at the end. Management did not concede, but proposed that, if the whole deal were accepted it would guarantee against compulsory redundancy for two years. The unions did not accept, citing more generous terms agreed between Usco and another partner. Continuing discussion, which merges from consultation into negotiation at this point (as noted earlier, the company is relaxed about fusion) led to Telecom accepting a period of five years and a 'sweetener' of £1500 for each staff member transferred.

'...developments may occur that are not directly attributable to the principal parties in the consultation'

A management 'sticking point' is clearly established and communicated. Consultation blurs into negotiation as a form of concession bargaining seeks to ease a way through this contentious area.

Job security discussions continued but were set back by a Usco announcement that about 200 of the lower level transferred jobs (50 covered by TUPE, 150 from the contract staff) would possibly be off-shored. Usco met with the lead union negotiator, who was opposed to this, but Usco would not guarantee there would be no redundancy. Usco did agree to secondment of the 50 for the duration of the project, with later redeployment back to Telecom, while the agency staff were given a commitment by Telecom that the site would be kept going, and the agencies themselves were satisfied that in these circumstance they could cope. The union concerned accepted this position.

Agreement at the top consultative level (senior management and union national officers and executive members) was reached in early May on the package. The white-collar union was prepared to accept, but the manual union Executive rejected the agreement, holding out for the right of transferees to return at the end of the contract. This led to further meetings first with the manual union and then both unions together, covering three areas:

i   A further session on the strategy for the benefit of the reluctant union Executive, to reduce their concerns.

ii A meeting with Usco senior management, who provided reassurance on continuity of employment intentions.

iii Telecom agreed that if Usco downsized, Telecom would seek opportunities for those affected to return to it – but continued to stop short of a *right* to return.

This package was accepted at union executive level and put to a ballot of employees affected, accompanied by a road show for the employees, working examples of individual situations. At this point it was discovered that the model tool used by Usco to calculate pensions was producing a shortfall in the expected figures. This seriously undermined staff trust and confidence in the deal, even when the use of the tool was withdrawn. One union continued with the ballot, achieved a 70 per cent turnout, which rejected the proposal with a narrow majority. The other union suspended the ballot until the problem was resolved – but both unions were seriously hostile at this stage, leading to threats of strike action.

It was decided that the date for implementation should be set back one month to allow time for the issue to be resolved through further reworking and consultation. Telecom found it necessary to significantly upgrade the amount it was to provide for the focused funding to cover shortfalls. Agreement with both unions was reached on this in late June and a second ballot was undertaken, supported by the provision of independent financial advice brought in to advise individuals on their positions. The membership of both unions narrowly accepted this.

The final stages prove to be among the most difficult. Two major setbacks are encountered: the miscalculation of the pension entitlements, and the off-shoring proposal by Usco, both of which seriously threatened to undermine trust in the relationships between the parties. The involvement of a third party (Usco) further complicates the picture with regard to trust – as we saw in Chapter 4, developments may occur that are not directly attributable to the principal parties in the consultation. In the end, after initial rejection, agreement was reached, but with narrow majorities, almost certainly reflecting continued misgivings among employees whose confidence and trust in the process would be shaken by the unexpected developments on pension calculations and off-shoring. These factors also increased the cost to Telecom, which was pushed to make additional concessions in order to achieve agreement on what was seen as a critical strategic development.

This case reveals some of the very real difficulties that a consultative process may encounter. It involved a critical need to maintain a running dialogue among the key players – a process of 'informed socialisation' maintained at different levels and on different issues throughout the protracted consultation. Formal meetings and presentations (information provision) were important but not sufficient in themselves. The companies can be criticised for not being clear and correct on the details of the pensions policy, which was obviously of vital importance to this group of employees. The complexity of the pensions issue called both for real expertise and an effective fusion of consultation and bargaining in order to reach a solution. Also, as in bargaining, the use of limited 'sweeteners' (but maintaining stances on matters of principle such as the denial of right of return to Telecom) to assist the process to move ahead was important.

Case 2: Communications

Key Features

This case concerns a major player in the UK communications sector. This group of companies, employing over 200,000, has had a troubled history of industrial relations for a number of years, making it increasingly difficult for the business to compete with growing competition. Pay and conditions are settled by national bargaining, but are commonly varied by local bargaining. In 2001 an independent review supported by the company and the unions – a powerful blue-collar union and a white-collar or management union, both with very high levels of membership – produced a report recommending the adoption of a partnership approach to both the business and industrial relations problems, with a strong focus on information flows and consultation with employees to counter historical problems of lack of trust. This partnership route was seen as the means of providing an organisation-wide, articulated consultative counterpart to lessen the confrontational bargaining culture.

2001–02: first steps to partnership

The Independent Report of July 2001 called for an end to the disastrous level of industrial action – official and unofficial – to provide a breathing space into which a new partnership way of working could be introduced. As a result, a moratorium was agreed on both management action on changes to working practices at local level without involving the national parties, and on threats of industrial action. A dramatic fall in days lost through stoppages was achieved in the following year, allowing progress to be made on the development of a partnership approach.

Rather than try to progress to a full partnership directly, the parties agreed to set up a national partnership board (NPB) and 14 local partnership boards (LPBs) on a pilot basis, after which the intention was to roll out LPBs at area level in March 2003. This would coincide with a proposed reorganisation reducing the number of areas from over 60 to 31. The aims of the NPB and the LPBs were to implement recommendations from the Independent Report, and to take on a consultative role, sharing strategic thinking, operational planning information, and seeking common ground. There would however be no scope for dealing with pay and conditions issues, which the unions saw as confined to the normal bargaining channels.

The NPB, which met monthly, comprised a Chair (the Chairman of the Independent Report), four senior management representatives, seven union officers (five from the manual workers union, two from the staff union), and a TUC representative. The LPBs each comprised four managers and eight area-level union representatives, with an external chairman, also meeting

> **'In such a large organisation...the ambition of effectively changing the prevailing culture and working practice through progression to partnership relations was likely to prove highly demanding.'**

monthly. A regional tier of boards was introduced on a pilot basis in three regions, having a co-ordinating role, sharing best practice developments, and supporting the work of the LPBs. Apart from the NPB, all staff reps were elected union members, not union full-time officers. Thus there was no role in the machinery for non-union employees.

The pilot LPBs gelled quite quickly: the participants were already well known to each other, and used to working and negotiating together. This made it easier to build on existing relationships, in contrast to the NPB where relationships needed to be developed. The NPB had less tangible issues to work on, making it difficult to develop communication on business issues and plans. But although experience was variable, some LPBs quickly moved to sharing information and discussion of plans, while others tackled softer behavioural and people issues, change activities or key people problems like bullying and communication. The advantages of bringing in a third-party chair at LPB level were acknowledged, especially given the introverted nature of the organisation, where 90 per cent of managers are appointed from within.

In such a large organisation, with a large amount of unfortunate historical baggage, the ambition of effectively changing the prevailing culture and working practice through progression to partnership relations was likely to prove highly demanding. Considerable attention was paid to the design to ensure both a national and local level of participation, but as might be expected, local take-up was uneven and the national body found it difficult to progress in the absence of a clear agenda at that level.

November 2002–2003: serious problems emerge

Practical difficulties soon emerged in distinguishing consultation and negotiation: the manual workers union was insistent that partnership boards must not get involved with negotiation. These difficulties were exemplified by a management proposal to introduce an

employee share-ownership programme, on which they consulted with the unions. The manual workers union wanted assurances that the programme would be *negotiable* since it saw this as affecting pay and conditions. This triggered other union complaints that management was initiating changes (on redundancy, harassment policy and managing absence) without union agreement. As a result, the union suspended its involvement in partnership in November 2002, withdrawing from the NPB, though some LPB activities continued. The continuation of the partnership in turn became an issue in impending elections for national officers, which were not due to be resolved until summer 2003.

Meanwhile, the future of partnership was on a knife-edge, underlining the 'fragility of partnership' and the difficulty of sustaining partnership relations. The activities of the pilot boards were curtailed and the planned rollout of LPBs across the country was shelved for the time being. The National Board continued to meet, and the manual workers union gave a dispensation to two members to continue their NPB involvement.

The tensions are now clear. From the business perspective, management sees an imperative need to make progress in turning the corner to profitability, but the historical baggage and power base of union–management relationships remain dominant influences, effectively bringing the limited progress to a halt. A key issue is the historical distinction in the business between consultation and negotiation, which the unions see as an essential protection for their bargaining activity and its scope. Consultation in this case is clearly viewed by the unions as a secondary channel, while management are seeking to upgrade the consultation mechanism to provide a more powerful and flexible form of employee voice.

Despite these setbacks, there were some positive signs. The NPB Chair produced a second progress report in Spring 2003. Where work was continuing at local level, there was positive feedback from participants, though with some frustration that full participation was suspended. Continuing without the manual union, by far the bigger union and critical to the activities of the boards was not a realistic option. However, new key players among employees – not always union representatives – were beginning to emerge. Senior management was still firmly supportive, seeing benefits in the achievement of reduced strike activity and improvements in business performance – the ultimate test.

Evaluation by the Partnership Support Group (based at Head Office and including union members) identified weaknesses in the performance of the consultative role by representatives who were more accustomed to a bargaining role. The average representative was in his mid-30s, 20 years out of school and with low educational qualifications. Consultation demands an ability to sit through presentation of plans, figures and detail, to which they were not attuned. As a result it was difficult to get engagement and rational debate on the issues, and there was concern about the representatives' ability to feed back accurate reports on outcomes to other members.

Management and unions agreed that there was a need for training to improve skills in presenting information and making information understandable (*how* information is best provided) and raising skills (literacy, numeracy, communication and leadership) of representatives (and employees generally). The manual workers union reviewed its own training programme in learning centres, mainly on procedures, tribunal representation, etc; but also to include leadership, representative functions, and communication; ie, more behavioural issues. There was a need also to address the problem that many employees (including managers) have a concept of 'leadership' that tends to be 'macho' or 'hero leadership', rather than the coaching and development aspects that are necessary.

The issue here is about the different skills and behaviour involved in negotiation and consultation, especially

where the business tradition has been one of hard distributive bargaining with what has remained a relatively militant and aggressive workforce. Recognition of this leads to deeper analysis of the differences and the way in which this could be tackled through training, particularly emphasising the behavioural aspects so critical to consultation and effective transfer of information.

A further issue emerged. At area level the LPB could be consulted by the area general manager on business plans for the next year; including elements of change, spending, job losses, etc, but the unions said this was not truly consultative since the plan was already prepared. Perhaps next year they could start earlier, and work with management to develop the plan.

But this, of course, raises familiar problems (which may not yet be fully recognised by representatives). If they develop a *joint* plan, they become responsible/ accountable for it, and are involved in ownership of the plan – which they may not want. Even if they do, their members vote for them each year and may not like what their reps have agreed, or see them getting too close to management, as a result of which they could be voted out. This could make it difficult to develop continuity within partnership; it also reflects immaturity in the representative's consultative role.

Some LPBs began to address this problem, looking for help from the Partnership Support Group which analysed training needs for managers and representatives involved in partnership working under three headings: informational (eg on implementation of agreements and procedures), behaviours implicit in partnership processes and values, and personal training (including influencing and persuading skills). (See Chapter 4, Table 6, p46)

Senior management recognised the need for support to be given to the regional and local boards. A specialist team from head office continued talking regularly to the management representatives about partnership as a way

> **'...expectations about consultation can quickly become disillusioned if the ground rules have not been mutually established and agreed.'**

of working, and means to involve union (and non-union) people locally. These steps reflect the following views:

i   that many managers were not buying in to the programme, preferring to see it as essentially structural reform, rather than the desired attitudinal and behavioural change, and

ii   that knowledge is building up about the possibilities of change and improvement for the individual worker, and this needs to be diffused more widely.

The issues here are the familiar ones of determining when is the appropriate time for consultation, and the roles, responsibilities and skills of representatives – on both employee and management sides. On the one hand, expectations about consultation can quickly become disillusioned if the ground rules have not been mutually established and agreed. Only experience on the ground will reveal whether that understanding has been achieved. Likewise, with regard to behaviour and skills, only experience will show up deficiencies and point to the need for a more thorough exploration of what types of training are necessary.

Postscript: 2004

In the Spring of 2004, the NPB Chair issued a third report, referring to the considerable change in personalities that had occurred in the previous year, both on the management and union sides. It observed:

'Few of the original partnership boards that were launched continue to meet, and it is now clear that this model will not work within [*Communications*]. Elsewhere, commendable work has been done jointly on supporting dignity and respect at work and lifelong learning initiatives. In recent months I have facilitated talks between [*Communications* and the unions] nationally and am encouraged by what I have seen. There

is an apparent willingness to find more productive ways of working together, and verbal support for the partnership principles that I have endorsed in previous reviews. All parties are committed to building closer understanding and to tackling the behavioural issues that have marred their actions in recent years. My principal recommendation is that joint working groups be set up to build on this work; these groups should work together to tackle the key issues that affect organisational relations between the company and the unions.'

This case serves as a reminder that not all attempts to build consultative structures and processes are guaranteed to be successful. It also demonstrates that the process of trying to build new structures and processes, especially in large organisations, is not a quick, 'one-shot' fix. In this case, management saw the development of informational and consultative procedures and processes as a key to developing partnership, improving industrial relations, and (critically) generating major improvements in business performance. The partnership path has proved difficult but progress has been made, and in the meantime there are positive signs, such as vastly reduced industrial action, hardly any of it unofficial, improved business performance (a return to profitability), and some swell of enthusiasm for the new approach among employees. The structure that has been created seems likely to be consistent with new legislative requirements, but the aspiration of partnership has not yet been properly established. But as well as structure, there needs to be a concern for process, and the skills and capabilities that good process will demand. This is well recognised by the organisation and the unions, and a specialist team is playing a key role in identifying what is needed and providing support to the area boards in a variety of ways. Training is only partly about providing information: both behavioural development and personal development seem critical to longer-term success.

'**The CIPD's Organising for Success research has found that major companies typically go through some form of reorganisation or strategic shift every three years.**'

Case 3: PowerCo

> **Key features**
>
> *PowerCo* is a major UK energy provider and distributor employing almost 15,000 workers in Britain and overseas. It recognises five unions and union membership is just under 60 per cent of UK employment. As detailed in our earlier report, the company altered its consultative and negotiating arrangements to match a change in corporate strategy and consequential reorganisation. (Beaumont and Hunter, 2003, pp 24–28). We are concerned here with one Division employing about 2,500. The new Divisional machinery was agreed and implemented from late 2002. It comprises three Joint Negotiating and Consultative Committees, covering three bargaining units organised by different trade unions: Engineering and Technical, Industrial and Admin/Clerical). The Company is relaxed about the fusion of consultation and negotiation in a single body, providing some continuity between the two activities (which proves important in this case). Below that level are Local Forums, which provide a form of local and job-related communication and consultation with employees, relating to the management of change.

Continuing strategic change

In 2002, a further strategic change was already being contemplated to improve customer service, to fit with longer-term investment strategy and conform with license obligations. This would move the business from a geographical to a functional form, reflected in a '5 pillar' model, comprising:

i   Control, restoration and repair (committed to restoring supplies to customers).

ii   Business Support.

iii   Distribution network investment.

iv   Connections.

v   Engineering and Transmission Operation.

This had major implications for job structures and terms and conditions, requiring a combination of consultation and negotiation. It also had implications for the consultative structure itself, as we shall see.

The CIPD's Organising for Success *research has found that major companies typically go through some form of reorganisation or strategic shift every three years. This is certainly true of this company over the last dozen years. If consultation and information are to play a real part in the business, it is likely that the structures and their operation will be subject to similar rethinking.*

Consultation: process and experience

One highly significant result of the new structure was to require more effective use of staff in Control, Restoration and Repair (CRR), which dealt with 25,000 network incidents per annum. Investigations had shown that only 40 per cent of these occurred in the normal working day (8 am–4 pm): the balance was handled through a combination of standby and overtime working, but it is clear that resources were not well matched with actual workload. To achieve better customer service and better matching of demand, there was a need for 24-hour network management and shift working arrangements for about 2,500 employees. No manpower reductions were envisaged.

This is clearly not only a major organisational change, but one that has strong business and employment implications. It was important to stress from the outset that no redundancy was intended (and indeed there was none.) The changes in working arrangements were not likely to be popular since they affected the personal freedoms of employees, would involve a loss of overtime earnings for many, and would involve staff in taking on wider geographical responsibilities.

January–April 2003: Clearly, such a major change would require consultation and negotiation. But before this process was formally started, in the first four months of 2003, employee representatives were involved in various workstream groups to begin to flesh out what the organisational changes would mean in terms of workloads and working arrangements. This permitted an early involvement of representatives at a stage when many of the issues were still very capable of being shaped by employee opinion and understanding of local issues.

May 2003: The first formal step was the announcement of the 5 Pillars Programme to the Joint Co-ordinating Council (the highest Divisional level for consultation) at the end of April, immediately followed by announcement to employees affected and a series of road show presentations across locations. A very detailed set of proposals and rationale for each functional pillar was presented by management, with the following timetable:

> ### Initial timetable for agreement
>
> **April/May 2003**: Communication to JCC and stakeholders (employees), including an outline of 'Next Steps' covering the allocation of personnel to the new functions, the emphasis on consultation, communication and negotiation throughout and appeal arrangements
>
> **June onwards**: negotiations
>
> **September**: formation of new pillars
>
> **December**: network centres established
>
> **April 2004**: structure implemented
>
> **June 2004**: full implementation.

Further consultation and negotiation was passed to the three Joint Negotiating and Consultative Committees in the Divisional machinery, which would be regularly updated on progress in the overall programme and would report back on their own progress to the JCC on a quarterly basis. There were in fact two main issues:

- the acceptance and detailed working of the new functional structure, which meant employees being re-allocated from a geographical to a functional unit, dependent on the sort of work they had principally been doing in the past twelve months. Appeals were allowed, but only 53 were progressed from a total of about 2,500 employees.

- The negotiation of terms and conditions of employment under the new working arrangements, which was probably the trade unions' main concern, but which could not be negotiated until the re-allocation had been decided.

The process would have been simplified had there been a single bargaining and consultative unit, rather than the three that were required to meet union traditions: two of the unions will not share a common bargaining table. This inevitably soaked up a lot of management time and effort in communication and consultation, and must certainly have raised in the minds of management a future agenda seeking to integrate these three committees.

December 2003–January 2004: At respective meetings of the Joint Negotiating and Consultative Committees, it was reported that significant progress had been made on the principal issues, including the transition from existing working practices and work patterns, and a package of measures would be recommended for moving into the 5 Pillars organisation structure. The detailed arrangements for 24-hour working remained to be settled. Minutes of meetings indicate that the consultative process had provided clarification on many issues and had led to modifications in management proposals in certain respects. Thus by early 2004, the main structural proposals had been accepted, but the terms and conditions issues remained to be finalised.

> **'This recognised the reality that formal consultation in itself is only one tool, which may not be sufficient in itself, and requires to be supported by other means of communication…'**

January–April 2004: Presentations were made to staff in a spread of depots, to report on the outcome of the consultation process and intentions to cover the remaining steps, particularly shift rotas and 24-hour working. The Local Forum level of consultation was now in full swing, with representatives being involved in discussions about the best solutions for standby and shift working for their areas. June still remained as the expected completion date.

Although the formal consultations were continuing and increasingly moving to a negotiation phase it is important to note that this was paralleled by a strong supporting programme of communication directly with employees and dealing with individual issues raised in appeal. This recognised the reality that formal consultation in itself is only one tool, which may not be sufficient in itself, and requires to be supported by other means of communication, particularly on issues that affect or concern the individual employee. The planned end-date for agreement and implementation is now looming, and the representatives show signs of concern that negotiation will not be completed in time – perhaps a subtle means of applying pressure to win concessions?

Hard bargaining in the three joint Negotiating and Consultative Committees now took place, and progressive implementation of the new arrangements began from late summer. However, in the case of the Engineering JNCC this was extended to October before agreement was finalised. The main issues were the actual percentage rate for shiftworking, and the hours and manning of the new shift systems. The substantial increase in shift working meant there was a decrease in the frequency of standby working, and this is where most concessions were made as compensation for the move to shiftwork.

November–December 2004: The re-organisation into functional areas and the reallocation of staff meant that the previous structure and membership of the local Forums were no longer appropriate. Changes in structure and personnel were agreed and implemented. It was also agreed that the working of the new structures and working arrangements should be kept under review at quarterly intervals, since these significant changes were likely to take some time to bed down and might need some detailed tuning in the light of experience.

Although many organisations prefer to separate consultation and negotiation, there may be advantages in fusion, as here. The joint negotiating and consultative committees were able to move smoothly from an essentially consultative mode towards a progressively bargaining mode as the issues shifted from the organisational change itself to the determination of the terms and conditions that would apply under the new arrangements. However, a single negotiating and consultative body would surely make for a less complex process.

The initial timetable was not achieved – despite the fact that the planned duration for such a major change was about 15 months. In the end, the solution was down to hard bargaining. Also, it is worth noting that it is accepted that such major changes may not gel instantly, and that there is value in a regular review of the new structural and working arrangements.

To underline the main point of this case, it is important to recognise that once an information and consultative structure has been put in place, this is not a once for all solution. Dynamic organisations will undergo changes in strategy and organisation on a recurrent basis, and when this happens, the consultative arrangements themselves may need to be reviewed and updated, if they are to continue to be relevant to significant business developments.

'**Consultative skills need to be developed on both sides; roles and responsibilities in consultation need to be clearly defined and mutually understood...– a key task for HR.**'

Summary of main learning points from the case studies

As noted at the start of this chapter, significant points have been noted as the narrative of the cases developed. It may be useful, though, to conclude this chapter with a reminder of the most important generic issues.

◘ *Timing*: particularly where the consultative issue is recognisably complex and potentially difficult, it is important that early intimation of proposals is provided. This step needs to be supported by good management preparation for disclosure with a clear presentation and rationale.

◘ *Continuing dialogue*: what was described as 'informed socialisation' helps both parties to define the respective sticking points and enable a problem-solving approach to be pursued. This may begin to merge consultation with bargaining – but only if both parties are content with this; in some instances the strong preference will be to maintain separation.

◘ *The unexpected will happen!*: key personalities will change, unforeseen difficulties will arise, and human error will lead to mistakes. The risk is that precipitate action in response to these events will do damage to the longer-term relationship which may be of greater value than the quick fix which sends the wrong signals and reduces confidence and trust.

◘ *Consultative skills* need to be developed on both sides; roles and responsibilities in consultation need to be clearly defined and mutually understood, as well as the agreed parameters of consultation – a key task for HR.

◘ *Consultation* is a key adjunct to strategic business development and organisational and workplace change. In turn, the drive for business performance gives consultation real purpose and importance.

◘ *Indirect consultation* through representatives needs to be supported by regular information to and communication with the whole employee workforce.

6 | Summary and conclusions

In this final chapter we:

◘ highlight the importance of addressing process as well as structural issues regarding consultation;

◘ outline in summary the key lessons we draw for practitioners from our work to date;

◘ revisit one of our cases in order to emphasise the need to continually monitor and adjust the process of joint consultation over time;

◘ identify the specific roles of the HR function in relation to the arrangements for information disclosure and consultation.

The focus of management attention: differing perspectives and implications

A number of our cases, particularly in the first stage of our research, had a prime focus on structural issues. That is, they were overwhelmingly concerned with issues such as the number of employee representatives, the appropriate constituencies of such representatives and the personal qualities of the representatives. This concentration is logical, understandable and indeed desirable as long as management recognises that this is only one aspect of consultation, which needs to be considered equally as a process ongoing over time. In our view such an appreciation of process was not always apparent among some of the management respondents we interviewed.

There were two major 'dangers' that we think were apparent here, and which we urge management (and indeed employee and union representatives) to guard against:

◘ A perception that if one can only get the structures right, then the necessary, underlying process of consultation will simply 'roll out' in a relatively straightforward, unproblematic way.

◘ A related view, that the key determinant of an 'effective' resulting process of consultation will be the election of employee representatives characterised by personal attitudes and behaviour which were variously labelled 'self-confident', 'leadership-orientated', 'pro-active' etc.

The underlying process of consultation is too important simply to be left to emerge over time. Instead, a lot of careful thinking, discussion and training needs to be given to help shape it in the desired direction. Furthermore, the simple concentration on employee representative attitudes and behaviours risks ignoring the full range of other influential factors (see Chapter 2), and tends to accord limited recognition to the fact that the employee representatives need to have a positive interaction process with their workforce constituents, as well as with the management representatives.

The second broad group of case studies here (although much less so in the first stage of the research) was one that readily appreciated the importance of the process of consultation. In such cases the major issues tended to be seeking to ensure an appropriate set of ground rules for consultation to help ensure that:

◘ the employee representatives worked well as a group (this was particularly the case if there were union and non-union employee representatives) and

> 'To eliminate completely all surprises in the rapidly changing context of so many organisations is, to say the least, a difficult (some would say impossible) task.'

▫ these employee representatives worked well with their management counterparts.

To achieve such ends the organisations in this second category were placing a great deal of emphasis on the role of training.

However, one needs to recall here the key message of our Engineering case in Chapter 4, namely that the 'across the table' perspective apparent in such cases is important, but is not the full story. This is because of the need to address and continually bear in mind the vulnerability of trust across the table to events that occur within the organisation that are beyond the table. As we shall see in the next section this is one of the key messages we draw on the basis of our research to date.

Our central message to practitioners

Throughout Chapters 3–5 we have provided at various points commentary on the lessons of a number of our cases. If we add these together and summarise them they all point in one direction: the establishment of a successful process of joint consultation (and its subsequent maintenance over time) requires:

▫ mutual agreement as to what the process of consultation should essentially embody and involve;

▫ seeking to ensure that potential organisational disruptions to this process should be minimised over time, and

▫ facing up to challenges as they occur to the initial process, dealing with these, and learning from them in a way that deepens and enriches the initial process, which should continue to develop and evolve.

In our view, the first step is essentially one of 'consulting about the nature of consultation'. That is, the designated employee and management representatives agree to sit down together to jointly design and agree the key, essential elements of a 'good and effective' process of consultation, informed by the existing guidelines . This first step is essential to help both shape and align the expectations of the two sides of the consultation table which are so important in producing the desired pattern of interpersonal and inter-role interaction that needs to be characterised by predictability, reliability and consistency. In particular management must be capable of providing clear-cut responses to employee representative views, and a clear justification for the final decision reached.

As the management and employee representatives interact over time, on the basis of these initially agreed ground rules, any likelihood of the initial basis of trust developing into one based on more of a shared identity with similarity of aims is unlikely to occur if the larger organisational setting is a source of 'passive resistance' and/or 'strategic shocks'. Such inconsistencies (perceived by the employee representatives) are likely to raise concerns about management's collective competency to organise and co-ordinate their own words and actions.

There is an analogy here with the 'no surprises' notion that is so prominent in current management thinking about how to conduct effective face-to-face performance appraisals and reviews. To eliminate completely all surprises in the rapidly changing context of so many organisations is, to say the least, a difficult (some would say impossible) task. However, what is clear is that the HR function, particularly at the senior level, has a major role to play in their interactions with their other managerial colleagues by seeking to minimise such surprises by heightening their awareness of just how sensitive a creature the joint consultation process is to such occurrences. This 'no surprises' theme is certainly prominent in one union's view of 'effective information and consultation' (see below).

A union view of effective information and consultation

◘ Information shared in a methodical and consistent way, enabling a shared knowledge base to be built up over time – a no surprises culture.

◘ The forum acts as a sounding board, where issues are raised, views are expressed openly and honestly and understanding grows.

◘ Everyone taking part is regarded by all as an equal and legitimate participant, enjoys the support of their colleagues, and is an effective participant.

Health warning: a good start is no guarantee of continual progress

To illustrate our third key message concerning the need to confront, deal with and learn from challenges over time we return to the case where we looked at how Drinks Co had sought to establish a mutually agreed set of ground rules for the process of consultation (see pp 29–31). At the time we obtained this information we believed that it

was one of the most impressive starts made by any of our cases. However, on our most recent visit to the organisation we found that the following issues and concerns had arisen in a half-day special meeting to finalise the constitution of the body, and in the first full-day meeting of the body:

◘ There had been some disagreement between the union and non-union representatives about who were to be representatives from the UK on the EWC.

◘ Issues were raised about one of the elected non-union employee representatives who since the election had been promoted further within the management grades of the organisation.

◘ A number of unfavourable comparisons were made with the extent and nature of support for employee representatives in this body compared to the EWC.

However, the major hotly-disputed issue was the closure of a small facility (involving some 12 employees). This was not on the agenda of the body because in management's view this was a subject for local, not national, level consultation (see p 30, Developing and defining the process of consultation); this view was not shared by the employee representatives.

In management's opinion, the employee representatives seemed to feel that their representative role required them to be fully-informed of all developments ongoing in the UK. Following the 'hostile and unproductive' first meeting of the council, a memo had been sent out from Human Resources (see below).

Drinks Co

UK Council – training workshop

Reflecting on the discussion at the last employee council meeting, I would like to suggest that we invest a little more time together as a group. I think it would be valuable for us to work through some of the business training that is available within the organisation so that we all have a chance to get more practice sharing opinions, challenging ideas constructively and generally have a bit more practice on some business issues that everyone will have an opinion about.

As a part of this I'd like to suggest we tackle head on the issue of 'competent business' and reach a shared understanding about what is a UK issue and what is appropriate for local consultation.

I would like to suggest we do this at a workshop. We offer the following training within the business and I'd be interested in what areas you would prefer to work on as a group so that we can shape the day. For example:

- Working in a group – team roles and personal styles.

- Conflict resolution.

- Change curve – how individuals cope with change.

- Practice tackling some live policy issues

where everyone will have a view – eg alcohol policy.

Some of you are seasoned debaters, but for others, this whole process might still seem daunting. By investing a little more time working together as a group, we can build a council that works well together and one where every member is confident debating issues and articulating constructive, though possibly opposing, views.

Regarding 'competent business', I'd like to suggest that each representative thinks about the topics, affecting all or a major part of our business, they would expect to discuss at the council that meet the current constitution. These could be real issues or scenarios that you might consider could possibly impact on our business.

By sharing our ideas on the topics we'd like to bring to the table we will be able to agree what is competent business and why, and this will help us all reach a common understanding.

Let me know if you would like us to arrange such a workshop and if you have specific training preferences that will help shape the workshop.

This example, combined with the experiences over time outlined in chapter 5, make clear that the process of consultation as it unfolds over time will almost inevitably encounter periodic events and challenges. Such events and challenges are double-edged. If they are successfully dealt with and do

> '...HR should view itself, and strongly convey this view to all others, as the guardian of the "all-important process of consultation".'

not damage the underlying process then that process is likely to be reinforced positively and hence deepened and enriched. Alternatively, if not dealt with substantively and/or handled with a perceived damage to the process then that process becomes at risk – with a resulting loss of commitment, confidence and trust. For practitioners, alertness to the double-edged nature of such challenges and events will require a capacity to monitor, learn and develop over time. For researchers, they point to the all-important need to conduct longitudinal case studies in which the 'process of consultation in action' is centre stage.

The role of the HR function

In our view, the cases presented in this report point to four separate, but inter-related, roles that HR professionals can and should play in relation to arrangements for information disclosure and consultation. First, as virtually all our cases have shown, HR has taken a lead role in designing new and reformed sets of arrangements; this said, we are conscious that our cases have very much involved larger, well-managed organisations, and we are aware of how many other organisations have, as yet, done relatively little in preparation for the implementation of the regulations.

The important point to make under this heading is that this role has (properly) involved a positive 'business case' being made for new and reformed arrangements (ie, it will contribute to improved larger organisational performance). This is necessary to ensure that such arrangements are not viewed as essentially a discrete, self-contained set of arrangements whose measures of performance are overwhelmingly seen to be HR-centred or dominated. As one HR manager put it to us,

consultation arrangements where all the action steps are on HR is not the way to go.

The second role concerns the issue of who are to be the management representatives on the arrangements? Again, in virtually all of our cases, a relatively senior and experienced HR professional was among the management representatives. As to who else should be the representatives of management our cases pointed to the existence and importance of a senior line management presence. This in our view was essential to ensure consistency with the 'business case' point made above, and to help signal the status and importance of the arrangements.

The third role, which will be one of the most difficult, but important, is to help minimise 'beyond the table' type announcements and behaviour which can damage the trust which is so essential to establish and maintain between the employee (trade union) and management representatives. Here we recommend that the mechanisms and forums which have been set up to establish a relationship between business strategy and HR strategy be continually utilised by senior HR professionals to emphasise and re-emphasise to senior line management colleagues just how vulnerable consultation is to 'strategic shocks'.

The fourth role is that HR should view itself, and strongly convey this view to all others, as the guardian of the 'all-important process of consultation'. This means that it should naturally take the lead in monitoring the effectiveness, development and sustainability of the process over time. But, at the same time, it must have the full support and assistance of line managers in general in implementing any necessary changes to reinforce, strengthen and deepen the processes; making sure (via both training and communication) that line

managers understand, appreciate and are aware
of what is going on in consultation will be
essential prerequisites in this regard.

In summary, a close, effective and sustainable
'partnership' between HR and line management is
an all-important prior step to having a close,
effective and sustainable process of employee
(union)–management consultation.

References

BEARDWELL, I. (1998)

'Bridging the Gap? Employee Voice, Representation and HRM', Chapter 9 in Sparrow, P. and Marchington, M. (eds) *Human Resource Management – The new agenda*. London: Financial Times/ Pitman Publishing.

BEAUMONT, P. AND HUNTER L, C. (2003)

'Collective Bargaining and Human Resource Management in Britain: Can Partnership Square the Circle?', in Kochan, T.A. and Lipsky, D.B. (eds), *Negotiations and Change: From Workplace to Society*. Ithaca: ILR Press, pp161–168.

BEAUMONT, P. AND HUNTER, L.C. (2003)

Information and Consultation: From Compliance to Performance. London: CIPD.

CULLY, M., WOODLAND, S., O'REILLY, A. AND DIX, G. (1999)

Britain at Work. London: Routledge.

DEPARTMENT OF TRADE AND INDUSTRY (2004)

Information and Consultation directive draft guidance. Available at www.dti.gov.uk/er/consultation/proposal.htm

FOX, A. (1985)

Man Mismanagement. London: Hutchinson, 2nd Edition.

GUEST, D.E. AND HOQUE, K. (1996)

'Human resource management and the new industrial relations', in Beardwell, I. (ed), *Contemporary Industrial Relations*. Oxford: Oxford University Press.

HUSELID, M.A. (1995)

'The impact of human resource management practices on turnover, productivity and corporate financial performance, *Academy of Management Journal*, Vol 38:3, pp 635–672.

KOCHAN, T.A. AND DYER, L. (1995)

'HRM: an American View' in Storey, J. (ed.) *Human Resource Management: a Critical Text*. London: Routledge.

LEWICKI, R.J. AND WIETNOFF, G. (2000)

'Trust and Trust Development and Trust Repair' in Deutsch, M. and Coleman, P.T. (eds), *The Handbooks of Conflict Resolution: Theory and Practice*. San Francisco: Jossey Bass, pp86–107.

LEWICKI, R.J., MCALLISTER, D.J. AND BICS, R.J. (1998)

'Trust and Distrust: New Relationships and Realities', *Academy of Management Review*, 23, pp438–458.

MARCHINGTON, M. (1989)

'Joint consultation in practice', in Sisson, K. (ed.) *Personnel Management in Britain*. Oxford: Blackwell.

MAYER, M., SMITH, A. AND WHITTINGTON, R. (2004)

Restructuring Survey: Stage Two. London: CIPD (draft).

NATIONAL CENTRE FOR PARTNERSHIP AND PERFORMANCE (2004)

Information and Consultation: A Case Study Review of Current Practice. Dublin: NCPP.

SARGEANT, M. (2001)

Employment Law. London: Pearson.

WOOD, S. (1995)

'The four pillars of human resource management', *Human Resource Management Journal*, Vol 5:5, pp 49–59.